The Random Book of…

JAMES

Well, I didn't know that!

All statistics, facts and figures are correct as of March 31st 2009.

Published By:

Stripe Publishing Ltd
First Floor, 3 St. Georges Place, Brighton, BN1 4GA

Email: info@stripepublishing.co.uk
Web: www.stripepublishing.co.uk

First published 2009

10-digit ISBN: 1-907158-04-9
13-digit ISBN: 978-1-907158-04-9

Printed and bound by Gutenberg Press Ltd., Malta.

Editor: Dan Tester
Illustrations: Jonathan Pugh (www.pughcartoons.co.uk)
Typesetting: Andrew Searle
Cover: Andy Heath

For my dad – my namesake – the most famous
James of them all, and also Clare, Emily
and Jessica, from a James who loves
them very, very much.

INTRODUCTION

Think of the Christian name James and what is the first thing that pops into your head?

No doubt most of you will consider a posh chauffeur whilst others may think of a disciple of Christ.

The name isn't restricted to rich people and religious followers…

If you trawl the pages of history the name crops up again and again. Sometimes that of a ruler of a great nation, other times as a leader of a great army, there's a James on every page of every history book… almost.

Movers and shakers from sport, film, literature and science all boast this classic and historical forename, a name that has been attached to some of the most distinguished people to have walked the planet.

There have also been some notable naughty people named James too, but every name has a few black sheep attached to it!

Here's to all the people named James out there. We salute you!

James Whittington – March 2009

JAMES THE NAME

James (pronounced Jaymz) is one of the most popular names in the world with over 4 million US men (which works out at around 3.318%) bearing the name. Meaning "the Supplanter" it was derived from the Hebrew name Jacob. The name Jayme is a very rare female variant on the name James. More popular deviations are Jim, Jimmy, Jamie and Jamesie.

Over the last eight years **James** has appeared in the UK Top Ten of baby boy first names but has begun to slip down the chart.

Year	James	Most Popular
2000	3th	Jack
2001	4th	Jack
2002	4th	Jack
2003	4th	Jack
2004	4th	Jack
2005	4th	Jack
2006	6th	Jack
2007	9th	Jack

In the United States James was the most popular boys name in 2000. Surnames that derive from **James** include Jameson, Jameston, Jamieson and Jamison.

Looking for a derivative slant on the name James? Let's ask our non-English speaking friends for help...

JAMES AROUND THE WORLD

Albania:	Jakup
Azerbaijan:	Yaqub
Belarus:	Jakub
Bulgaria:	Yakov
Catalan:	Jaim
Croatia:	Jakov
Czech:	Jakub
Denmark:	Jakob, Jeppe
Esperanto:	Jakobo
Faroe Islands:	Jákup
Finland:	Jaakko, Jaska, Jimi
Galician:	Xaime
Hawaii:	Kimo
Hebrew:	Ya'aqov
Holland:	Jacob
Hungary:	Jakab
Iceland:	Jakob
Irish:	Séamus, Séumas
Italy:	Giacomo
Japan:	Yakobu
Korea:	Yagop
Latin:	Iacobus
Latvia:	Džeimss
Lithuania:	Jakūbas
Malaysia:	Yacob
Malta:	Ġakbu, Jakbu
Norway:	Jakob, Jeppe
Poland:	Jakub, Kuba
Romania:	Iacob, Iacov
Russia:	Якоb (Yakov)

Scotland Gaelic:	Seumas
Serbia:	Jakob or Jakov
Slovakia:	Jakub, Kubo, Kubko
Spain:	Diago
Sweden:	Jakob
Ukraine:	Якіb (Yakiv)

RHYMING SLANG JAMES

Traditional Cockney rhyming slang works by taking two words that are related through a short phrase and using the first word to stand for a word that rhymes with the second.

Jim Fenner – a tenner
Jimmy Riddle – piddle, to urinate
James Brown – to frown
James Dean – keen
Jim Bob Babs – crabs

JAMES IN ACTION

Multi-Oscar winning director **James Cameron** is best known for his mega-budget special effects-laden movies such as *Titanic* (1997*)*, *True Lies* (1994), *Terminator 2: Judgment Day* (1991), *The Abyss* (1989) and the gung-ho sci-fi sequel shocker *Aliens* (1986). His first credited directorial job was on the movie *Piranha 2: The Spawning* (1981) which is, according to Cameron, "The finest flying piranha film made". Despite this inauspicious start he is one of the most successful writer/directors in Hollywood today, which is lucky as he's been married five times. In 2007 *Total Film* voted him the 37th Greatest Film Director of All Time.

Hard man **James Coburn** (1928-2002) was named after his father and possessed the middle name Harrison. In his later years Coburn suffered from severe rheumatoid arthritis that, for a time, put a halt to his acting career. He was also one of many famous faces that appeared on the cover of the Paul McCartney and Wings album Band On The Run. Other celebrities on the sleeve were Christopher Lee, Michael Parkinson, Clement Freud, John Conteh and Kenny Lynch. Coburn returned to movie acting in the 1990s and won the Best Supporting Actor Oscar for his performance in Paul Schrader's film *Affliction*.

James Whale (1889-1957) was a British-born director who took America by storm in the golden age of cinema by delivering three of the most iconic and truly horrifying movies of all time; *Frankenstein* (1931), *The Invisible Man*

(1933) and *Bride of Frankenstein* (1935). Bill Condon's bio-pic about Whale, *Gods and Monsters* (1998), cast Sir Ian McKellen in the role of the director.

DISTINGUISHED JAMES

Respected, multi award-winning actor **James Earl Jones** has loaned his vocals to many different media including giants such as news channel *CNN* and *Disney* but he is most famous for voicing the character of Darth Vader in the *Star Wars* saga. He wasn't George Lucas's original choice, though. Orson Wells topped the list.

James Neville Mason (1909-1984) played a number of army characters during his cinematic career but was a lifelong pacifist. During World War II he refused to sign up for action stating that he was a conscientious objector. This caused a rift in his family that took years to heal.

His ashes were laid to rest, 16 years after he died, at a cemetery in Corsier-sur-Vevey, the same Swiss burial ground as Charlie Chaplin. Allegedly the delay was due to a lengthy family battle over his estate. Until then his ashes had been held in a vault in Geneva.

America's favourite good guy **James Stewart** (1908-1997) served in the United States Air Force and rose to the rank of brigadier general. Mostly remembered for his role in Frank Capra's *It's A Wonderful Life* (1946) the film actually failed at the box office and was only rediscovered when it went out of copyright, thus falling into the public domain and shown regularly on US television. Though nominated for five Oscars he received only two; one for his performance in *The Philadelphia Story* (1940). The other

was an Honorary Award in 1985. His middle name was
Maitland.

⇒·◆·⇐

Irish-born heartthrob **James Nesbitt** became UNICEF
UK Ambassador in 2005. As an advocator for children's
rights his main aim is to bring to the public's attention the
suffering of youngsters around the globe. UNICEF (**U**nited
Nations **I**nternational **C**hildren's **E**mergency **F**und) was
established in 1946 to help aid children affected by the
horrors of World War II.

Want an insight into popular culture? Look no further than
writer **James Wolcott**. He has a monthly column in *Vanity
Fair* that comments on the topics of the month. He has also
written two novels, *The Catsitters* (2001) and *Attack Poodles and
Other Media Mutants* (2004).

Jamie Foxx (born Eric Marlon Bishop in 1967) is one of
America's finest entertainers. A self-trained stand-up comic,
he joined the TV show *In Living Color* in 1991. He released
his first album Peep This in 1994 and won an Oscar for his
performance as Ray Charles in the movie *Ray* in 2004.

The Scots are known for their resilience to pain
(apparently), none more so than goalkeeper **Jim Blyth**.

During his 1982-83 season at Birmingham, Jim fractured his arm in several places but kept on playing for 70 minutes against Sunderland. His team still won 2-1.

If you fancy a chat with a real entrepreneur then invite **James Donal Wales** (born 1966) around for a cup of tea and a custard cream. He was one of the creative forces behind the online encyclopaedia, Wikipedia and according to his creation his nickname is Jimbo.

JAMESES YOU MAY MEET IN HEAVEN

Legendary runner **James Cleveland Owens** (1913-1980), better known as Jesse, was an Olympic athlete who, in 1936, won four gold medals in track and field events, much to the annoyance of Adolf Hitler. He got the tag Jesse when his schoolteacher misheard him say his initials, J. C.

Winger **James Yates** (1871-1922) enjoyed a colourful footballing career which began in 1891 at Burnley, for a season. He went on to play for a further eight clubs, finishing his career at Salisbury City in 1909. Sadly, after retiring from football he had to find work and ended up at Southampton Docks where he was employed as a labourer. His deteriorating health cost him his job and he committed suicide in 1922.

The Nooksack tribe hail from the north-western part of Washington called Deming in the USA. One of their chiefs in the late 1800s was Chief Yelkanum Seclamatum who was also known as **Chief Jim**.

The first American to win an FIM (Fédération Internationale de Motocyclisme) title was **Jim Pomeroy** (b. 1952) in 1973. He was killed in 2006 when his Jeep rolled in Yakima, Washington.

MUSICAL JAMES

The singer/songwriter, poet and all round trouser snake rock-god **Jim Morrison** had the middle name Douglas. He lived his short life to the full regularly binging on alcohol and drugs and was found dead in a bath in Paris, France in 1971. He was only 27, the same age Jimi Hendrix and Kurt Cobain were when they passed away. No autopsy was performed paving the way for countless theories from fans on the cause of death. The surviving members of The Doors – Robby Krieger, John Densmore and Ray Manzarek – released two more albums after Jim's death. Other Voices (1971) and Full Circle (1972) both failed to connect with fans and the group disbanded in 1972. In 1978 The Doors recorded music for *An American Prayer*, a collection of old poetry readings Morrison recorded shortly before his death.

Australian critic, columnist and essayist **Clive James** (b. 1939) has collaborated with musician Pete Atkin over the last four decades composing lyrics for Pete's music. James has also released a collection of his poems entitled *Opal Sunset – Selected Poems 1958-2008*.

Indie group **James** were originally called Venereal and the Diseases, then changed to Volume Distortion, then Model Team International. After going under the title of Tribal Outlook the name changed to **James** in 1982. It was taken from group member **Jim Glennie**, not because he had delusions of grandeur but simply because they all felt it fitted and would lead the audience to believe they were just one person and not a group. Their first gig 'James (Not A Poet)' happened in August of that year.

Born **James Todd Smith** in Queens, New York in 1968, rap star, actor and producer **LL Cool J** made his first record aged just 16. His tag is an acronym for **L**adies **L**ove **C**ool **J**ames.

Godfather of Soul **James Brown** (1933-2006) probably had more nicknames than any other artist. Favourites include 'The Hardest Working Man in Showbusiness', 'The Godfather of Soul' and 'Mr Dynamite'. His body of work is in constant use and I Got You (I Feel Good) (1965), Get Up, I Feel Like Being a Sex Machine (1970) and Living in America (1984) are some of the most played songs on American radio.

Brown was name checked in the song Genius of Love in 1981 by Tom Tom Club. His high energy stage performances earned him huge respect from his peers and in 2003 he was made the first 'Secretary of Soul and Foreign Minister of Funk' by US Secretary of State General Colin Powell, though a job description was not drawn up.

Electro warrior Gary Numan was actually born **Gary Anthony James Webb** on March 8th, 1958.

Jim Diamond and Tony Hymas, under the name of
PhD, had one hit single with the track I Won't Let You
Down, in 1982. It reached number three in the charts
but Jim had better success as a solo artist with tracks
such as I Should Have Known Better (number 1 in 1984)
and Hi Ho Silver (number 5 in 1986), which was the
theme to the hit ITV series *Boon*, which ran from 1986
until 1992.

Blur bassist turned columnist **Alex James** has also worked
with several other notable artists including Marianne
Faithful and Sophie Ellis Bextor. Unfortunately, he will
probably be remembered for his association with Fat
Les, a temporary group consisting of artist Damien Hirst
and actor Keith Allen. Their World Cup single Vindaloo
reached number two in the UK chart in 1998. They would
release another two singles; Naughty Christmas (Goblin
in the Office), which reached number 21 in 1998 and
Jerusalem charted twice in 2000, reaching number 10 and
number 55.

Of all the musical James's, **Jimmy Page** is probably the
most highly respected. He started his professional musical
career in The Crusaders, in 1962, and, disliking the
fluctuating workload, he became a session musician and
appeared on a number of hit singles including Twist and
Shout with Brian Poole and the Tremeloes (1963), As Tears
Go By (1964) with Marianne Faithful and Lulu's version of
Shout (1964).

After initially turning down a position with them, Page joined The Yardbirds in 1966 and stayed with the group until 1968 when after several member changes they morphed into Led Zeppelin. The band officially split in 1980 after the death of drummer John Bonham. Page was awarded the OBE in 2005 in recognition for his work with poor children in Brazil. He had joined up with charity Task Brasil to open Casa Jimmy, a safe house that has helped hundreds of needy children.

JAMES AT THE TOP

In 1961 **James B. Parsons** become the first African-American District Court Judge. He went on to become the first African-American Chief Judge of a Federal Court in the U.S. District Court of Chicago in 1975.

Aptly named **James Richburg** is one of the world's most successful professional poker players. A player who takes part in most formats he has won, or been highly placed, in several events at the annual World Series of Poker tournaments.

James Sadler (1753-1828) was the first Englishman to make a balloon ascent in England. It is estimated that on October 4th, 1784 he reached a height of around 3,600 feet. But, he was not the first person to perform such a feat; Tuscan Vincent Lunardi took flight in his balloon a month earlier. Although Sadler would go on to invent the table steam engine his life was darkened by the death of his son in 1824 during a balloon ride.

James W. Gibson transformed the fortunes of Manchester United in 1931 by paying off more than £30,000 worth of accumulated debt and becoming chairman. Gibson was a manufacturer of army uniforms and helped to rebuild Old Trafford after it was heavily bombed during World War II. He also appointed Matt Busby, who used to play for Manchester City, as manager in 1945. Busby's tenure lasted 28 years and his first signing was **Jimmy Murphy**.

JAMESES YOU PROBABLY WOULDN'T ASK AROUND FOR TEA

The **Jim Rose Circus** (a circus sideshow) first came to
the public's attention during the Lollapalooza Tour of
1992. The original line-up included The Enigma (originally
named Slug) who would eat anything, Bebe the Circus
Queen who would rest on a bed of nails whilst weights were
placed upon her and Torture King who walked on a ladder
of swords. Both Jim and Enigma appeared in an episode of
The X-Files entitled Humbug in 1995.

Australian-born drifter **James Miller** was accused
alongside Christopher Worrell for what became known as
the Truro Murders. Between 1976 and 1977 the deadly
pair slaughtered seven innocent women and their reign of
terror only came to an end because Worrell was killed in a
car accident in 1977. Miller's mind descended into further
madness and he let slip one evening in a bar about Worrell's
activities. He was tried in 1979, found guilty of six of the
seven murders and given a life sentence for each of the
killings.

NOVEL JAMES

Schoolboy wizard and all-round good guy **Harry Potter** has the middle name **James**. It comes from his father who was killed, along with his mother, Lily, by Lord Voldemort. His birthday is July 31st, 1980, the same date, but not year, of Potter creator J.K. Rowling.

Born in Dublin, Ireland **James Augustine Aloysius Joyce** (1882-1941) became one of the most respected writers of the 20th century penning classic texts such as *Ulysses* in 1922 and *Finnegan's Wake* in 1939. He suffered poor eyesight from birth but a doctor in 1894 actually told him not to wear glasses. Joyce did not wear spectacles for a decade and as a result had to undergo eye surgery to try and correct his problems.

Horror writer **James Herbert** has sold over forty two million books worldwide since his first novel *The Rats* (1974) was published. Four of his tomes have been turned into movies; *The Survivor* (1981), *The Rats* became *Deadly Eyes* in 1982, the paranormal *Haunted* appeared in 1995 and shaggy dog story *Fluke* a year later. None of them retained the horror and atmosphere of their source text.

Sir James Matthew Barrie (1860-1937) gave the world *Peter Pan* in 1904. The classic play of the boy who never grew up became an instant hit. In 1929 Barrie gave all royalties and rights to Great Ormond Street Hospital.

A sequel, *Peter Pan in Scarlet* was written by Geraldine McCaughrean and released in 2006.

Many assume that P.D. James is a male, but in fact the author of the Adam Dalgliesh thriller books is called **Phyllis Dorothy James**.

One of Hercule Poirot's most enduring associates is **Chief Inspector James Japp**. A class contrast to the Belgian detective, Japp only appeared in ten of Agatha Christie's *Poirot* original novels but is a regular in the long-running ITV series (1989-2009) which stars David Suchet as the clever detective and Philip Jackson as Japp. Suchet himself played Japp in the 1985 TV movie *13 at Dinner*, which starred Peter Ustinov as the moustachioed smarty-pants.

American novelist **James Norman Hall** (1887-1951) wrote the classic seafaring text *The Mutiny on the Bounty* in 1932 but few would know that this was actually the first part of a trilogy. The other two are *Men Against the Sea* and *Pitcairn's Island*, both released in 1934.

James Henry Trotter is the main character in Roald Dahl's book *James and the Giant Peach*, which was originally published in 1961. Dahl fronted the ITV anthology series *Tales of the Unexpected* for two seasons – 1979 and 1980 – adapting some of his own short stories. These twist-in-the-tale pieces continued without him until 1988. The famous naked dancing lady title sequence was accompanied by a haunting theme composed by Ron Grainer who was also behind the themes for *Doctor Who*, *The Prisoner*, *Man in a Suitcase* and *Steptoe and Son*.

JAMES ON THE EDGE

Jim Bridwell was born in 1943 and went on to become one of the world's most respected climbers of his generation. He has first ascended countless climbs and helped to form the Yosemite National Park Search and Rescue Team. Many of his rescue techniques have become standards.

Bouldering is a form of rock climbing where the person doing the task uses very little equipment omitting to use even the basics such as a helmet. Think of the opening scene from *Mission: Impossible II* (2000) or the form of climbing from *Cliffhanger* (1993) to get the idea.

Top ranking boulderer **Jim Holloway** is noted for his creative and self-titled names for easy, medium and difficult routes. The 6ft 4ins. climber retired from bouldering after the cerebral nerves in his legs were damaged.

The first American to climb Mount Everest was **Jim Whittaker** in 1963. He would also lead the first American ascent of K2 in 1978. His twin brother, Lou, is also a climber. Jim is now a highly successful motivational speaker.

JAMES HAS LEFT THE BUILDING

Hollywood heartthrob **James Dean** was born on February 8th, 1931, and became one of the most recognisable icons of the 20th century... but only completed three movies before he died in a car accident on September 30th, 1955. His first acting job was a small role in a Pepsi commercial. American band The Eagles recorded the song James Dean for their 1974 album On The Border.

Canadian actor **James Montgomery Doohan**, who played Chief Engineer Montgomery Scott in the *Star Trek* series and associated spin-off movies, was a Vietnam vet who lost his right middle finger in combat. Doohan wrote his autobiography *Beam Me Up, Scotty* in 1996. He died in 2005 aged 85 as a result of a combination of Alzheimer's disease and pneumonia. There have been a number of attempts to launch a sample of his ashes into space; none have been successful, as yet, although some have orbited the earth and returned to solid ground.

Born on May 8th, 1913 in Hancock Street, Newcastle, South Africa to show business parents, Sidney Joel Cohen changed his name to **Sid James.** His began his working life as a very successful hairstylist using his haircutting ability and gentle patter to charm his female clients. He longed to be an actor and carved himself a solid career in theatrical productions and got his big break in radio and TV versions of *Hancock's Half-Hour.*

Though a huge success, Hancock was worried that viewers had begun to think that they were a double act and Sid was written out. But Sid went onto greater things and appeared in 19 of the Carry On film series, cementing his place in British comedy history. He died on stage at the Sunderland Empire on April 26th, 1976.

Extrovert King of Funk **Rick James** (born James Ambrose Johnson, Jr.) was the nephew of Melvin Frank, a member of soul group The Temptations. He was signed as a staff writer to Motown in the 1960s but it wasn't until he released his fifth album, Street Songs, that critical recognition came his way. The Grammy Award nominated album also had a nominated single, Super Freak, a track that was heavily sampled on the MC Hammer single U Can't Touch This in 1990. Rick's rock 'n' funk lifestyle – he was a drug user and had, by his own admission, slept with thousands of women – took its toll on his body and he was hospitalised on many occasions. He died on August 6th, 2004 leaving behind a funky legacy and a son named Tazman.

Political writer **James Arthur Baldwin** was born in 1924 into great poverty. Not knowing his father, James began preaching aged just 14. He became one of the most respected African-American writers of his generation. His themed essays and books mirrored what was happening in America at the time and covered topics such as sexuality and civil rights. His release *The Fire Next Time* (1963) is credited as paving the way for his position at the Advisory Board to the Commission for Racial Equality. He died of stomach cancer in 1987.

Though remembered fondly for his role of professional spiv Private Joe Walker in the gentle comedy *Dad's Army*, **James Beck** (1929-73) was a respected character actor starring in such shows as *Coronation Street*, *A Family at War* and *The Troubleshooters*. The role of Walker was actually written by co-creator Jimmy Perry for himself. In a recent stage show revival, Leslie "Dirty Den" Grantham played the character. Despite being one of the youngest members of the aging *Dad's Army* cast, Beck was one of the first to die at the age of just 44.

ARISE, KING JAMES

King James I of Scotland (1394-1437) was the son of
King Robert III and after marrying Jane Beaufort held his
coronation on May 2nd, 1424. A respected scholar and man
of the arts, he enjoyed writing poetry. His published work
includes *The King'i Quair (The King's Book)*, his most famous
collection. His life was cut short when he was murdered on
February 20th, 1437. His son, James II was only seven at the
time so Scotland was governed by regents for a period of time.

A regent is someone chosen to act as a Head of State when
the appointed person is not old enough, too ill or otherwise
unable to complete or perform his or her duties.

King James II of Scotland (1430-1460) was only seven
when he came to the throne so wasn't able to take full
command until he was 18. Due to a birthmark he was given
the name of 'James of the Fiery Face' and, sadly, he was
killed when a cannon he was firing exploded during the
Siege of Roxburgh Castle. He was only 29.

King James III of Scotland (1451-1488) was, like his
father James II, crowned at an early age. His reign began
when he was just 9-years-old. Like many of the Kings of
Scotland his death was not a natural one; he was wounded
at the Battle of Sauchieburn but was then stabbed to death
by a person posing as a priest!

King James IV of Scotland (1473-1513) came to power, aged 15, and is famous for wearing an iron belt as a penance for causing the death of his father. Known for his non-royal duties such as poetry writing, womanising (he fathered at least three illegitimate children), his skills at foreign languages and dentistry! He miscalculated an invasion of England and died at Flodden Field on September 9th, 1513.

King James V of Scotland (1512-42) was the youngest James to become King, being only 17 months old. He eventually took on full Royal duties when he was 15 and is one of the few nobles of the time to die from natural causes. After his uncle, Henry VIII, invaded his borders he died from nervous exhaustion and depression. Sadly this was only six days after his daughter Mary was born. He was 30 years of age.

King James I of England and Ireland and VI of Scotland succeeded Elizabeth I in 1603. He died at the ripe old age of 58 – which was good for its time – six years after the passing of his wife Anne of Denmark. He wrote two books on monarchy and government; *The Trew Law of Free Monarchies* and *Basilikon Doron*.

On November 5th 1605 one Guy Fawkes – also known as Guido Fawkes – was discovered in a cellar in the Houses of Parliament. Fawkes (1570-1606) was precariously placed on top of 36 barrels of gunpowder. He was tortured for several days – until he eventually blabbed on his co-conspirators – and was eventually hanged, drawn and quartered. His corpse was then dragged through the streets of London, just to make sure he'd learned his lesson.

GRAPHIC JAMES

Garfield the Cat creator **Jim Davis** unleashed the greedy moggy in 1978 and the strip has gone on to be syndicated worldwide. It is estimated that over 200 million people read the cartoon every day. This is good for a guy who gained the lowest point averages whilst studying at Ball State University. He is not alone as American talk show host David Letterman also scored the same low mark.

Jim Bamber is well known for his motor sport cartoons that have appeared in various car-racing periodicals since 1983. He lampoons all the famous F1 drivers not by drawing their caricatures but by giving them all full-face helmets with their names written on them. He puts this novel idea down to "inherent laziness".

James Andrews (1801-1876) is one of the most famous botanical artists of the 19th century. He also spent his time teaching ladies the fine art of painting.

A mixture of TV show *The Avengers* and the *James Bond* novels, *Modest Blaise* first hit comic strips on May 13th, 1963. Co-created by artist **Jim Holdaway**, with long-term working partner Peter O'Donnell, the story of a sexy but deadly female spy was an instant hit. Italian beauty Monica Vitti played the lead role in the movie version from 1966. It didn't have the same impact as the comic strip and fans had to wait decades until 2004 for the next movie, *My*

Name Is Modesty: A Modesty Blaise Adventure. This also flopped and lead actress Alexandra Staden never played the role again. A TV pilot was made in 1982 but a series was never commissioned.

James David Hudnall was the creator of the comic book series *Harsh Realm*, which was adapted for TV by *X-Files* creator Chris Carter. It only lasted nine episodes with the first three being broadcast originally on Fox, an American TV network. US viewers had to wait to see the other six on the Fox-owned channel, FX, months later.

Though he began his professional career as a letter engraver and then a portrait painter, **James Gillray** (1757-1815) became one of the most famous caricaturists and satirists of his time. Most of his pieces were aimed at George III and Napoleon. His later years were dogged with misfortune; his eyesight began to deteriorate and there was no method of correcting the defect. He began to drink, sank into deep depression and even attempted suicide. He descended into madness but was looked after by the person who had published and sold his work, Hannah Humphrey. His work is much sought after by collectors and has fetched sums of up to £10,000.

MAGICAL JAMES

British-born magician **James Freedman** has many
tricks up his sleeve. An accomplished pickpocket, he has
earned the legend: "The Man of Steal". James also acts as
a magical advisor, working on films such as *The Illusionist*
(2006) and *The Brothers Bloom* (2007) as well as being
pickpocket advisor on Roman Polanski's *Oliver Twist* (2005).

American magician **James Ward Marshall** (1919-2005)
changed his name to Jay and became one of the country's
most respected performers. He is credited as being the first
act to open for 'Old Blue Eyes' Frank Sinatra when he first
performed in Las Vegas. His famous sidekick 'Lefty' was
constructed from a white glove with rabbit ears attached.

Professional sceptic and debunker **James Randi** (real
name Randall James Hamilton Zwinge) became interested
in conjuring when he suffered a bicycle accident, which saw
him housed in a body cast for 13 months. He spent his time
digesting conjuring books and went on to forge a successful
career and once upset Uri Gellar stating he was just a
magician, like himself. Gellar tried to sue but it was thrown
out of court. Randi also has an asteroid named after him:
3163 Randi.

STAND-UP JAMES

America's second favourite talk show host **Jay Leno** (James Douglas Muir Leno) was born in Scotland in 1950 and moved to the United States aged 11. He began his career in stand-up concentrating on observational comedy and soon progressed to TV and movies. He succeeded talk show legend Johnny Carson as host of *The Tonight Show* in 1992 and is an avid collector and restorer of classic cars and motorcycles. His dyslexia doesn't appear to have held him back at all.

Vaudeville star and comedian **James Francis Durante** (1883-1980) – the Schnoz to his friends thanks to his rather large nose – has inspired many cartoon characters to talk or imitate his distinctive vocal style, which became known as "language butchery". Spike the Bulldog from many Tom and Jerry cartoons is a prime example. His 1969 hit Make Someone Happy appeared on the soundtrack to the Tom Hanks movie *Sleepless in Seattle* (1993) and the twenty-first episode of season five of *Frasier* (1998) was called *Roz and the Schnoz*.

Irish comedian **Jimmy Cricket** (born James Mulgrew) became a household name in 1981 when he reached the finals of ITV talent show *Search for a Star*. With his trademark Wellington boots – marked L and R but worn on the wrong feet – turned-up hat and catchphrases "c'mere" and "...and there's more" his family-friendly comedy made him a star. Before he shot to fame he worked as a Pontins blue coat where he met his wife, May. They have four children; Dale, Frankie, Jamie and Kate. Kate is carving a career as a stand-up whilst Frankie left the comedy business to become a priest.

Controversial old-style comedian **Jim Davidson** failed an audition for the role of the Artful Dodger in the movie *Oliver* in 1968. Fame soon came when he won ITV's *New Faces* in 1976. His stand-up content was always near-the-knuckle but did become more PC as his TV work increased. This included the sitcoms *Up The Elephant and Round The Castle* (1983-1985) and *Home James!* (1987-1990), and presenting game shows *Big Break* (1991-2002) and *The Generation Game* (1995-2002). Jim is a strong supporter of British Forces performing many times to troops in action. In 1997 he won The Variety Club Of Great Britain Showbusiness Personality Of The Year award.

James Campbell is behind the Comedy4Kids show and claims to be the only stand-up comedian whose act is specifically aimed at children.

Jim Tavaré is the only comedian on the circuit to use a double bass as part of his routine. Rarely playing the instrument during his act his style of humour has been compared to the late, great Tommy Cooper.

Rubber-faced Canadian-born jester **Jim Carrey** (born 1962) is best known for his high budget big screen appearances in movies such as *The Mask* (1994), *Batman Forever* (1995) and *How The Grinch Stole Christmas* (2000). He started his career as a stand-up comedian at Canada's Yuk Yuk Club in 1979 and his first movie *Introducing… Janet* (also known as *Rubberface*) was two years later.

CHILDREN'S TV JAMESES

Cult favourite *Jamie and the Magic Torch* (1976-1979)
came from the famous Cosgrove Hall Animation Studios,
the place that also gave us *Dangermouse*. Written by Brian
Trueman it lasted 39 episodes and concerned young Jamie,
a boy who would shine his torch onto his bedroom floor to
open a magical portal into Cuckoo Land, a place populated
by surreal and bizarre characters such as Officer Gotcha,
Wellibob the cat and Bully Bundy. It also had a theme tune,
from Joe Griffiths, that you could play air guitar to!

High flying hand-drawn action came in the form of **Jimbo
and the Jet Set**, a series of 25, five-minute cartoons that were
shown on BBC 1, originally in 1986. Soaring in from the same
people that brought you *Penny Crayon* (1989) and *The Family Ness*
(1983) it paved the way for other animated planes including
Budgie from Sarah Ferguson, the then Duchess of York.

Fan-dabi-dozi Scottish double act The Krankies (in real life
husband and wife Ian and Janette Tough) first met in 1965
at the Glasgow Pavilion Theatre. They created an original
comedy routine with Ian playing a father figure and Janette
as **Jimmy**, his naughty yet lovable wayward son. Getting
their big break in 1978 when they won the Club Act of
the Year award, The Krankies soon became mainstays on
children's television, appearing throughout the 1980s on
shows such as *Crackerjack* as well as their own programmes,
The Krankies Klub (1982-1984), *Krankies Electronik Komik* (1985-
1987) and *Krankie Television* (1990).

In 1977 **Sally James** became the first female co-presenter of cult children's show *TISWAS* (**T**oday **I**s **S**aturday **W**atch **A**nd **S**mile, though some say the **S** stands for **S**ee) and her good looks and often sexy clothing made her a hit with older viewers too. Alongside Chris Tarrant they would gunge, soak and splash top stars of the day including Motorhead, Eddie Kidd, and Olivia Newton-John. Sally became lead presenter in 1981 when Tarrant left to front *O.T.T.* (**O**ver **T**he **T**op) an adult version of the show that launched in 1982. Neither programme lasted very long after this. Other presenters on *TISWAS* included Lenny Henry, Bob Carolgees, John Asher and John Gorman.

James is the name of one of the main characters from the original Pokémon series that began in 1998 and ended in 2006. James was part of Team Rocket alongside Jessie and Meowth whose task was to try and steal Ash Ketchum's collection of Pokémon animals. Three actors in the British edition of this Japanese favourite, Ted Lewis, Jimmy Zoppi and Eric Stuart, have voiced the whiny and pretty useless character.

Mega-brain boy genius **Jimmy Neutron** possesses the middle name Isaac. Created by John A. Davis, the CGI (computer-generated imagery) creation is voiced by Debi Derrberry, a singer songwriter who has also appeared in movies including *Free Willy* (1993), where she was the stunt double that rode the tame whale. Neutron's name is derived from James Chadwick and Isaac Newton.

The Random Book of...

EAST END JAMES

EastEnders was the brainchild of Julia Smith and Tony Holland and was first broadcast on BBC1 on February 19th, 1985. The soap opera, set around a traditional part of the East End, was designed to be a grittier soap than those at the time and its storylines produced some record-breaking audiences.

OAP favourite **Jim Branning** (John Bardon) was Dot Cotton's (June Brown) second husband after her original fella Charlie (Christopher Hancock) died in a car crash. Dot was Jim's second wife; his first, Reenie, died before the character of Jim was introduced.

Suave but sinister **James Willmott-Brown** (William Boyd) become Britain's number one baddie in the soap. Not only did his own bar The Dagmar take away most of the Queen Vic custom, Willmott-Brown forced himself upon Kathy Beale (Gillian Taylforth). He is now residing at Her Majesty's pleasure, Kathy left the Square and actor Boyd moved into post-soap stardom obscurity.

Sexy doctor Fred Fonseca joined the soap in 1999. Played by **Jimi Mistry** he didn't seem to enjoy his time as Dr Legg's replacement and left after only a year.

With a permanent scowl and a just as miserable partner, Martin Fowler (**James Alexandrou**) has had a hard life. In the real world James dated his co-star Kara Tointon, who plays Dawn Swann, and has progressed into theatre work.

One of the newest characters to join the Square is Liam Butcher played by **James Forde**. He is the sixth actor to play the character of Liam.

ALL ROUND JAMESES

Jimmy Nail (born James Michael Aloysius Bradford
in 1954) began his showbusiness career fronting the
band *The King Crabs*, often wearing a dress and boots
on stage. A welder by trade, he shot to fame in the TV
series *Auf Wiedersehen, Pet* (1983-1986 and 2002-2004)
as Oz (real name Leonard Jeffrey Osbourne). This led
to a recording career that began with a cover version of
the Rose Royce classic, Love Don't Live Here Anymore,
in 1985. He went on to pen his own songs hitting the
number one spot in 1992 with Ain't No Doubt. He
played the lead role in *Spender* (1991-1993), wrote and
starred in two series of *Crocodile Shoes* (1994-1996), and
appeared in the movies *Danny Champion of the World*
(1984), *Morons from Outer Space* (1985) and *Evita* (1996),
alongside Madonna.

James Francis Cagney (1899-1986) was most famous
for the hard guy gangster roles he played in the 1930s
and 1940s. He was also an accomplished song and dance
man who performed in chorus lines early in his career.
Allegedly, he was the target for the mafia during his
time as President of the Screen Actors Guild although
he never said "you dirty rat" in any movie. He is name
checked by Tom Waits on the song Invitation to the
Blues (Small Change, 1999). Also snood wearing, 80s
electronic keyboard wizard Nik Kershaw wrote the song
James Cagney for his 1986 album Radio Musicola.

James L. Brooks has a list of credits to his name that reads like a comedy greatest hits collection. He is a writer, producer, director and screenwriter behind such shows as *Mary Tyler Moore*, *Taxi*, *The Tracey Ullman Show* and *The Simpsons*. He won three Oscars in 1983 for his movie *Terms of Endearment*; Best Director, Best Picture and Best Writing-Screenplay Based on Material Adapted from Another Medium.

Jim Dale was one of the most accomplished artists to appear in the *Carry On* series of films. From an early age he knew he wanted to be an entertainer and studied many different dancing genres and performed in amateur shows. Aged 17, he became Britain's youngest professional comedian. A change of career after a two-year stint in the Royal Air Force came when he became George Martin's first artist and he had a string of hits with Be My Girl reaching number 2 in 1957. In the late 1960s he turned his talents to acting with critically acclaimed roles in *The Winter's Tale* and *A Midsummer Night's Dream*. He would return to theatre and in 1973 picked up several awards for his Broadway show *Scapino*.

Jim is an in-demand voiceover artist and has loaned his vocal talents to the range of Harry Potter audio books for US audiences. But his eleven outings in Carry On films are what he is famous for:

- *Carry On…Cabby (1963)*
- *Carry On…Jack (1963)*
- *Carry On…Spying (1964)*

- *Carry On...Cleo (1964)*
- *Carry On...Cowboy (1965)*
- *Carry On...Screaming (1966)*
- *Carry On...Don't Lose Your Head (1966)*
- *Carry On...Follow That Camel (1967)*
- *Carry On...Doctor (1968)*
- *Carry On...Again Doctor (1969)*
- *Carry On...Columbus (1992)*

Incidentally, Jim Dale was born in Rothwell –
Northamptonshire – which is the surname of Talbot
Rothwell, the man who wrote – between 1963 and 1974 –
what many consider to be the finest of the *Carry On* series.

ARISE, SIR JAMES

Now then, now then, ladies and gentlemen probably the most famous James to be knighted is cigar-chomping, charity championing **Sir Jimmy Savile OBE**. Born James Wilson Vincent Savile in Leeds on October 31st 1926 and one of seven children, he became a Bevan Boy during World War II and had various careers including hospital porter, club manager and wrestler. On January 1st 1964 he introduced the first ever edition of *Top of the Pops* and is one of the few people to have appeared on *This Is Your Life* twice. His most famous show *Jim'll Fix It* (1975-1995) was a television series where children, and sometimes adults, would write in with their greatest wishes and Jim would make them come true. His most famous guest was Peter Cushing who asked Jim to fix it for a rose to be named after his late wife, Mary. Now more famous for his charity work, he continues to generate millions for worthy causes. How's about that, then?

Classical flute player **Sir James Galway** was born in Belfast in 1939 and is credited as bringing classical music to the masses. In his career he has played alongside such luminaries as Henry Mancini, Ray Charles and Roger Waters and has sold over 30 million records. He received an OBE in 1979 and was knighted in 2001. In 1995 he was awarded the Outstanding Contribution to Classical Music award at the Classic Brits.

Next time you're enjoying a hot cuppa from a Thermos flask think of **Sir James Dewar** (1842-1923), the man who made it possible. Scottish-born Dewar was researching low temperature phenomena and needed to store liquid gases. As a result, he constructed the first double-walled vacuum flask. Dewar also invented the smokeless explosive cordite and was knighted in 1904. The name Thermos was sold to three independent companies in 1907.

SECRET AGENT JAMES

James Bond creator Ian Lancaster Fleming (1908-1964) wrote his first Bond novel, *Casino Royale*, in 1953. He went on to pen 12 Bond books in total along with two collections of short stories. Bond is described as being 183cms in height and weighing 76kg.

Other authors who have written official James Bond books are:

- Kingsley Amis: *Colonel Sun* (writing as Robert Markham)
- John Gardner: *License Renewed, For Special Services, Ice Breaker, Role of Honour, Nobody Lives Forever, No Deals Mr Bond, Scorpius, Win Lose or Die, Brokenclaw, The Man from Barbarossa, Death is Forever, Never Send Flowers, Seafire, Cold.*
- Raymond Benson: *Zero Minus 10, The Facts of Death, High Time To Kill, Doubleshot, Never Dream Of Trying, The Man With The Red Tattoo.* Also wrote three short stories, three film novelisations, two computer games, a role-playing game, a reference book and an unproduced stage play based on *Casino Royale.*
- Sebastian Faulks: *Devil May Care*
- John Pearson: *James Bond – The Authorised Biography*

In 2005 Charlie Higson began a range of Young Bond novels aimed at children, set in the 1930s and filling us in on Bond's past. Titles so far have been *SilverFin* and *Blood Fever*.

Blockbusters quizmaster Bob Holness was the first actor to play the character of James Bond; it was for the radio play *Moonraker* in 1956. Barry Nelson had played Bond in the TV episode *Casino Royale* in 1954 as part of the American series *Climax* but his Christian name was changed to Jimmy, and Bond had been turned into a CIA agent.

On the big screen there have been 22 official James Bond movies (meaning they were made by EON Productions) and six James Bonds:

- Sean Connery: *Dr No* (1962), *From Russia With Love* (1963), *Goldfinger* (1964) *Thunderball* (1965), *You Only Live Twice* (1967) and *Diamonds Are Forever* (1971)
- George Lazenby: *On Her Majesty's Secret Service* (1969)
- Roger Moore: *Live And Let Die* (1973), *The Man With The Golden Gun* (1974), *The Spy Who Loved Me* (1977), *Moonraker* (1979), *For Your Eyes Only* (1981), *Octopussy* (1983) and *A View To a Kill* (1985)
- Timothy Dalton: *The Living Daylights* (1987) and *Licence To Kill* (1989)
- Pierce Brosnan: *Goldeneye* (1995), *Tomorrow Never Dies* (1997), *The World Is Not Enough* (1999) and *Die Another Day* (2002)
- Daniel Craig: *Casino Royale* (2006) and *Quantum of Solace* (2008)

There have been two un-official big screen outings for James Bond:

- *Casino Royale* (1967) was a spoof that had seven actors playing a character named Bond and five credited directors.
- *Never Say Never Again* (1983) saw Sean Connery return to the title role, and was partly financed by the MFI Furniture Group.

PLACES WITH JAMES IN THE TITLE

The oldest but probably least known Royal Park is **St. James's Park**. Established in 1532 by Henry VIII and situated in central London, it is home to The Mall and is surrounded by three notable buildings; St James's Palace, the Houses of Parliament and Buckingham Palace, and covers 58 acres.

Another **St. James' Park** can be found in the north-east and is home to Newcastle United Football Club. Originally built in 1892, it was updated in 1998 into an all-seater ground with a capacity of 52,387, the third largest club ground in England.

James Bay is an area of water that can be found on the southern tip of Hudson Bay, Canada. It is named after voyager **Thomas James** who travelled to the area in 1631 but it was actually first discovered by Henry Hudson in 1610.

James Ross Island is situated at the north-eastern side of the Antarctic Peninsula and was discovered in 1842 by **Sir James Clark Ross**. It was not named until 1903 when Otto Nordenskiöld charted the area and named it in his honour.

In Florida you can journey to the **St. James Bay Golf Course**, which offers a luxury golfing experience!

JAMES – THE MOVIES

Jesse James (1939)

Two horses were killed in this very romanticised version of the Jesse James legend, which led to the tightening of the American Humane Association presence on movie sets. Starring Henry Fonda as Frank James, and Tyrone Power as Jesse James, it tells the story of two brothers who turn to robbing and looting to avenge their mother's death. Jess is shot and killed by one-time friend Robert Ford (John Carradine) in the back. A sequel *The Return of Frank James* arrived in 1940. There have been other Jesse James movies including; *Jesse James Under The Black Flag* (1921), *Jesse James The Outlaw* (1921), *Jesse James* (1927), *Days of Jesse James* (1939), *The True Story of Jesse James* (1957), *American Outlaws* (2001) and more recently the Brad Pitt feature *The Assassination of Jesse James by the Coward Robert Ford* (2007).

One of the more obscure ones is *Jesse James Meets Frankenstein's Daughter* (1966) where the cowboy hides in Frankenstein's castle and witnesses his friend's transformation into a monster. Directed by William Beaudine it was made back-to-back with *Billy the Kid Versus Dracula*.

Ever-evolving actress, singer and professional wig wearer Cher (real name Cherilyn Sarkisian) released the song Just Like Jesse James as a follow up to her international hit If I Could Turn Back Time. Both came out in 1989.

James (1979)

Little is known about this ten-minute short from prolific
director Laird Sutton, apart from that it was made for the
National Sex Forum. Other titles he directed were *Rich and
Judy* (1971), *Touching* (1972) and *Visions of Raspberry* (1979).

James (1997)

This Irish short was written, directed and produced by
Dermot McNevin and was his only cinematic release. It
stars Jamie Cohen in the title role. The piece was backed by
the Dun Laoghaire Institute of Art, Design and Technology
(DLIADT).

James (1999)

Also known as *Kick* this is a *Billy Elliot* kind-of-a-film, which
stars Russell Page as Matt Grant, a rugby player who
wants to become a ballet dancer. He grabs his chance by
auditioning for a role in Romeo and Juliet, ignoring the
pressures from his rugby team and his dancing partner
commitment. You can probably guess how it ends.

Strange James (2004)

This Australian movie centres on a young adult who relocates
to be away from his violent and abusive stepfather. Then it
all goes a bit weird as he experiences strange hallucinations
in his new surroundings. Written and directed by David Reid
this has been his only production to date.

James (2005)

This action adventure movie was the first production from director Rohit Jugraj. Shot in India with Hindi dialogue, the film follows James (Mohit Ahlawat), a hard-arsed boxer, who finds employment working the doors of nightclubs in Bombay. He rescues a young lady from being assaulted but opens up a can of worms as the attacker is related to thugs who "own" the police.

I KNOW THE FACE BUT NOT THE NAME

Scottish-born actor **James Finlayson** (1877-1953) began his cinematic career in early silent comedy shorts but found fame playing stooge to Laurel and Hardy, appearing in many of their most memorable moments such as *Pardon Us* (1931) and *Way Out West* (1937). His thick moustache and "D'oh" exclamation to camera made him famous.

Another Scottish actor, bearded **James Robertson Justice** (1907-1975), remained in the UK and in middle age quickly became typecast, playing the character of an upper-class parent or executive who looks down on all around. Best moments were in *Doctor in Clover* (1966) and *Chitty Chitty Bang Bang* (1968).

Though appearing in countless movies and TV shows, classically trained actress **Geraldine James** OBE is probably most famous for being the lactating mother character to David Walliams's Harvey, the man who is still fed from the breast in *Little Britain*.

Remembered now more for his elaborate moustache rather than his acting, **Jimmy Edwards** (1920-1988) was a comedy performer who became a household name in the 1950s and 1960s. His shows, which included *Whack-O! Seven Faces of Jim* and *More Faces of Jim* gained huge audiences. He was also known for his radio work on *The Glums*.

He shot to fame as kindly farmer Hoggett in the charming movie *Babe* (1995) but **James Cromwell** had been around for a piggin' long time before kicking off his cinematic career in the spoof comedy *Murder by Death* (1976). He has gone onto great critical acclaim in movies such as *Star Trek: First Contact* (1996), *LA Confidential* (1997) and *The Green Mile* (1999).

Pouring imitation coffee all day doesn't seem like a fun way to make a living but that's what **James Michael Tyler** did from 1994 till 2004 in the TV sitcom *Friends*. Tyler played Gunther, the manager at Central Perk whose crush on Rachel Green helped make him the most recurring character on the show, apart from the six main actors.

Kentucky-born actor **James Best** played bumbling Sheriff Rosco P. Coltrane in the hit TV series *The Dukes of Hazzard* from 1979 to 1985.

NOT REALLY A JAMES

Jimi Hendrix: Born Johnny Allen Hendrix on November 27th 1942, he was renamed James Marshall by his father later in his life. Apparently, Jimi was expelled from one school for holding the hand of a white girl. He died on September 18th, 1970, aged just 27, but the cause of the death remains a bit of a mystery. Popular myth is that he choked on his own vomit. He died the same year as singer-songwriter Janis Joplin, who was also only 27.

Jim Bowen: Born Peter Williams, his stage name comes from his adopted title James Whittaker and changed again when he married. He took his wife's maiden name of Owen and added 'B' and plied his comedy trade through the northern comedy clubs eventually getting his big break on ITV's *The Comedians* in the 1970s. But it's his 14 years as presenter of cult Sunday night game show *Bullseye* that made him a household name. His catchphrases "look at what you could have won", "stay out of the black and in the red, you get nothing in this game for two in a bed" and "BFH (**B**us **F**are **H**ome)" became legendary.

Controversial movie writer and director Abel Ferrara, he of *Driller Killer* (1979) and *Bad Lieutenant* (1992) fame used the pseudonym **Jimmy Laine** when he directed an unmentionable porn movie.

McMillan and Wife star **Susan St. James** was actually born Susan Jane Miller on August 14th, 1946.

Composer and producer Kinuyo Yamashita creates soundtracks and sound effects for the computer games industry, mainly on horror and fantasy titles such as *Castlevania*, *Buffy the Vampire Slayer* and *Knightmare III: Shalom*. She has been credited in the past by the name **James Banana**.

Author Alice Bradley Sheldon wrote under the pseudonym **James Tiptree, Jr.**, a name which was inspired by a label she saw on a jar of marmalade. She did this so her science fiction writing was taken on content alone, without causing debate on whether the female gender could write decent sci-fi. She also used the name Raccoona Sheldon. Sadly towards the end of her career Sheldon's husband's health deteriorated and in an act of love she shot her beloved partner and herself. They were found hand in hand in bed on May 19th 1987.

The James Tiptree, Jr. Literary Award Council was set up in her honour to acknowledge science fiction and fantasy writing that "expands or explores our understanding of gender" and to seek out work that is "thought provoking, imaginative and even infuriating" from both female and male writers.

ACCIDENTAL JAMES

James Levine is one of the most respected pianists and conductors of the age. He is credited for transforming the Metropolitan Orchestra into one of the finest ensembles around. In 2006 he fell off stage during an ovation injuring his shoulder.

Metallica guitarist **James Alan Hetfield** had his fair share of incidents. He once received forty stitches in his head after a shooting accident; has fractured both left forearm bones, in which two metal plates had to be inserted; fallen off his skateboard breaking his wrist and survived a bus crash that killed fellow band member Cliff Burton. He also received second-degree burns when a pyrotechnic effect went off too close to him.

On August 6th, 1883 **James Burton** became one of the very few men who had to be hanged twice. Condemned to death for the murder of his wife Elizabeth, he was readied for the long drop but one of his arms caught on the rope behind his back during the first try so the gallows had to be re-set and (unfortunately for him) it worked the second time.

Religious James

The most famous version of the Bible, **The King James Bible** was first produced in 1611 though the translation into English began seven years earlier in 1604. Over fifty scholars worked on the piece but it came a cropper in 1631 when a printing error crept into the holy publication. In Exodus 20:14, one of the Ten Commandments stated: "Thou Shall Commit Adultery". How many Christians followed the instruction is uncertain.

James was one of the twelve apostles who followed Jesus during his time on Earth. He was the son of Zebedee, brother of John – who also became a follower and hailed from Galilee. James and John were apparently given the surname "Sons of Thunder" or "Boaenerges" by Jesus.

There was also another James in the line-up, **James son of Alphaeus**. He is often referred to as James the Less.

It has been interpreted that Jesus had four brothers; **James**, Joseph, Simon and Judas, but some argue that these were his cousins. Jesus also allegedly had sisters but the Bible doesn't refer to any of these by name.

The James Ossuary is an infamous burial box (an ossuary is also known as a bone box) that was found in a private collection of artefacts in 2002 that bore the inscription "James, son of Joseph, brother of Jesus".

Obviously it caused ripples throughout the religious community and a team of 14 experts was assigned to check the authenticity of the inscription. In 2003 it was deemed a forgery.

It was tough being a Christian in the old days and one saint that can vouch for that is **St. James Intercisus**. He was slowly sliced into 28 portions (Intercisus is Latin for "cut into pieces") because he refused to apostatise (when a Christian refuses to give up their faith) and the torture began from his fingertips. He was eventually beheaded in 421AD and his feast day is November 27th.

Often depicted holding a chalice in his right hand with a snake inside trying to slither out is **St. James of the Marches** (1391-1476). The image is supposed to represent the heretics that tried to poison him. Pope Benedict XIII canonised him in 1726.

For twelve years **James McLoughlin** (1929-2005) was the Roman Catholic Bishop of Galway. His time ran from 1993 until 2005 and he was ordained by Pope John Paul II.

Kildare and Leighlin have had six James's as bishop; **James O' Gallagher** 1737-1751, **James Keefe** 1752-1787, **James Doyle** from 1819-1834, **James Walshe** 1856-1888, **James Lynch** 1888-1896 and **James Moriarty** who became bishop in 1991 and is still in charge.

JAMES IN SPACE

James's that have formed part of Space Shuttle crews over the years:

James Charles Adamson: Missions – STS-28 and STS-43

James Philipp Bagian: Missions – STS-29 and STS-40

James Frederick Buchli: Missions – STS-51C, STS-61A, STS-29 and STS-48

James Donald Halsell Jr.: Missions – STS-65, STS-74, STS-83, STS-94, STS-101

James McNeal Kelly: Missions – STS-102 and STS-114

James Hansen Newman: Missions – STS-51, STS-69, STS-88, STS-109

James Anthony Pawelczyk: Mission – STS-90

James Francis Reilly II: Missions – STS-89, STS-104, STS-117

James Douglas Adrianus van Hoften: – STS-41C and STS51-I, nickname is "The Ox"

Other notable James's in space include:

James Benson Irwin (1930-1991): Apollo 15 crew and eighth man to walk on the moon.

James Arthur Lovell Jr.: Commander on Apollo 8 mission in 1968, the first mission to enter lunar orbit and of the infamous Apollo 13 mission of 1970. Said the immortal line, "Houston, we've had a problem".

James Alton McDivitt: Gemini 4 and Apollo 9 missions.

CHECKMATE JAMES

James Mason (1849-1905) was born in Ireland, his real name is not known and his adoptive parents relocated to the USA in 1861. Several special sequence chess moves have been named after him including the Mason Variation and the Mason Gambit. During his career he wrote several books on the game, which were translated and published around the world.

Robert James Fischer became the first player from America to make a living from playing chess. A gifted and natural competitor he won many titles including the US and World Championships. Bobby, as he was known, suffered from multiple phobias including glaring lights and became obsessed by hidden cameras and came unstuck in 1992 when he ignored a US sanction not to play in Yugoslavia. He remained in Iceland until his death in 2008.

James Eade is probably the most famous player-writer around at the moment, mainly thanks to his best selling book *Chess for Dummies*.

Scottish player **James Macrae Aitken** was his country's champion ten times from 1935 to 1965. He played a massive part in World War II by working at Bletchley Park trying to decode the German Enigma machines. He died in 1983 aged 75.

JAMES TO A TEE

Scottish-born **James Alexander Barclay** only played golf at an amateur level and found his career working in the oil industry. When he retired he became curator of the golf museum section of the Royal Canadian Golf Association, wrote numerous books on the subject of golf, and was inducted into the Canadian Golf Hall of Fame in 2008.

James Martin Barnes (1886-1966) was born in Cornwall but found fame in the US where he became a professional golfer, earning himself the nickname Long Jim due to his 6ft 3ins. frame. His record of 'largest winning margin' at the 1921 US Open of nine strokes was not beaten until 2000 when a young golfer named Tiger Woods won by fifteen strokes.

American **James Benepe III** won only one official PGA Tournament, the 1988 Beatrice Western Open. He now earns his living selling jet fuel for a large company.

As well as being a professional golfer, **James Braid** (1870-1950) was also a golf architect who is credited with designing the 'dogleg' hole seen on many courses. He won the British Open five times.

The first golfer to win the Masters three times was American **James Newton Demaret** (1910-1983). *Golf Digest* named him the 20th Greatest Golfer of All Time in 2000.

Jim Furyk credits his father for his trademark "looping" golf swing, which has earned him the nickname "The Grinder". Mike Furyk never told his son to change his unconventional, but natural style, and Jim went on to become one of golf's greatest players equalling the record for the lowest 72-hole score to win his first championship.

Controversial golfer **Mark James** has led a colourful golfing career. In 1979 he was fined after the Ryder Cup for "contempt of authority" and when he became European captain in1999 left out Nick Faldo and Bernhard Langer from the team. In his first book *Into the Bear Pit* he confirmed the rumour that he placed a good luck message for the squad from Faldo into a bin. He won his battle over testicular cancer in 2000 and returned to golf the very next year.

JAMES ON THE PITCH

James Peter Greaves, Jimmy to his friends, played for England 57 times and became the country's third highest scorer. After four seasons at Chelsea (1957-1961) he transferred to AC Milan but left after just 14 appearances. Returning to native soil he began his legendary run at Tottenham Hotspur (1961-1970) but developed an alcohol problem during the 1970s. He returned to the limelight as a football pundit, and along with Scottish football legend Ian St. John fronted *Saint and Greavsie* for ITV for seven years.

Jimmy Montgomery made 623 appearances as goalkeeper for Sunderland AFC from 1960 until 1977, a club record. His double save during the 1973 FA Cup Final against Leeds United – where Sunderland won 1-0 – is often referred to as one of the greatest saves ever made. He never played for England.

Nottingham Forest player **James Perch** was once sent off for apparently head-butting Newcastle's Sacha Stephenson during a game.

JAMES AND FAMILY

Happy Days star Scott Baio (Chachi Arcola) has two cousins also in the acting profession; **Jimmy** and Joey Baio.

James Broderick is the father of *Ferris Bueller's Day Off* star Matthew Broderick. He appeared in classic American TV shows *Gunsmoke*, *Fantasy Island* and *Family*.

Jim Corr is the only male member of the drop dead gorgeous Irish family band The Corrs and, as well as playing guitar and providing backing vocals, he is also the oldest. His sisters in the band perform the following musical duties: Andrea, the youngest, provides lead vocals and plays the tin whistle; Caroline sings backing vocals and performs on drums and many other instruments while Sharon performs backing vocals and plays the violin.

James Belushi, the chubby faced actor in such lightweight pieces as *Curly Sue* (1991), *K9* (1989) and *K-911* (1999), is the younger brother of John Belushi (1949-82). John died tragically young, aged only 33, after a lethal dose of cocaine and heroin.

Actor John Voight is well known as being the father of Angelina Jolie but he is also the dad of actor-producer **James Haven** (sometimes known as James Haven Voight). His work includes appearances in *Breaking Dawn* (2004), *Stay Alive* (2006) and the TV series *CSI* (2004).

Hollywood character actor **James Whitmore**, famous for his role of bird-loving prisoner Brooks in *The Shawshank Redemption* (1994), is the father of actor/director **James Whitmore Jr**.

JAMES ON THE ROPES

George Smith hanged **James Owen** alongside George Thomas on April 11th, 1840. Smith was a hob-nailer (also known as a shoe maker) before he took up the gruesome occupation. The Owen Thomas double hanging was his first job. Smith was famous for wearing a top hat and a white smock when he was working. William Calcraft trained Smith, one of the most famous hangmen this country has produced.

From 1884-1891, **James Berry** (1852-1913) performed over 130 hangings and is famous for not only hanging five women, but also for being the hangman who tried and failed to hang John Lee. Lee became known as "the man they could not hang" and was reprieved after three attempts to hang him failed. All equipment was checked and when Lee was away from the gallows the trap door worked perfectly. Berry was also one of the few hangmen who could read and write and produced two books; *My Experiences as an Executioner* and *Hangman's Thoughts Above the Gallows*.

James Billington (1847-1901) succeeded James Berry as executioner and after a time was assisted by his own sons; Thomas, William and John. Billington committed the first hanging of the 20th century.

Over a period of just two years (1817-1819) hangman **James Botting** proclaimed that he had performed 175 executions. This fact has yet to be verified.

JAMES ON THE CATWALK

One of the oldest shops in London is **James Lock and
Co. Hatters, Ltd** which was established in 1676. Situated
in James Street it is steeped in hat history; for instance,
in 1850 a hat was created at the shop for a Mr. William
Coke. Mr. Coke wanted a piece of headwear that would
guard and protect the heads of his gamekeepers. Designed
by Thomas and William Bowler, "The Coke" hat soon
became known as "The Bowler" and a legend in attire
was born. The shop boasts that a postcard was delivered
to the property addressed "The Best Hatters in the World,
London". Do you think success went to their heads?

Another James who has a career in hats is **James Coviello**.
Bloomingdale's and Neiman Marcus picked up his first range
and he has also created fashions for runway shows.

Ex-*Casualty* star **James William Forbes Redmond**
started his showbiz career as a model when he was spotted
by a scout from Calvin Klein whilst working in Milan
in 1994. After taking therapy for a speech impediment,
James began his acting career in TV soap *Hollyoaks* in 2000
playing Rory 'Finn' Finnigan, tried presenting in 2002 on
SM:TV, and joined the *Casualty* team in 2003 as John 'Abs'
Denham, leaving in 2008.

AHOY, JIM LAD – JAMES AT SEA!

Probably the most famous James to sail the seven seas was **James Cook** (1728-1779), a gifted navigator and explorer who clocked up many nautical firsts. Born in Marton, Yorkshire he joined the Navy in 1755 and soon rose through the ranks. In 1768 he captained *The Endeavour* on a voyage to Tahiti and it was during this time that he helped to combat scurvy by ensuring there was fresh fruit and vegetables on board, as well as pickled goods and fresh milk from the boat's goat. Cook sailed around the world twice and was the first European to land in New Zealand. He died aged only 50 after being stabbed by a native in Hawaii. A statue of Cook stands in Greenwich, London.

American captain **James Lawrence** (1781-1813) gave birth to a naval cry that is still in use today, "Don't give up the ship!" *Star Trek* fans should take note that he sailed on the *USS Enterprise*, a schooner built in 1799.

The boat Sir Ernest Shackleton (1874-1922) used to navigate across 800 miles of the most barren terrain on Earth, namely the Antarctic, was the *James Caird*.

OK, a bit of a cheat, but there's also **Captain James Hook** who appeared in J.M. Barrie's *Peter Pan*! Also, **James Saxon** provided the voices for the revived series of *Captain Pugwash* in 1997, which had originated forty years earlier.

It is an urban myth that the series contained naughty innuendo in its characters names. Pugwash's Christian name was Horatio.

The blockbusting movie trilogy, *The Pirates of the Caribbean*, has a character called **Admiral James Norrington** played by Jack Davenport.

NOBEL JAMES

The Nobel Prize is an international award that is given to high achievers in the fields of chemistry, physics, physiology or medicine, literature, peace and economics. Established in 1901 – though the economics prize wasn't introduced until 1968 – those who receive the honour also receive a personal diploma, some cash and a medal.

Chemistry
James Batcheller Sumner (with John H. Northrop and Wendell M. Stanley) – 1946
Donald James Cram (with Jean-Marie Lehn and Charles J. Pederson) – 1987
Elias James Corey – 1990

Physics
James Franck (with Gustav Ludwig Hertz) – 1925
James Chadwick – 1935
Leo James Rainwater (with Aage Niels Bohr and Ben Roy Mottelson) – 1975
James Cronin (with Val Logsdon Fitch) – 1980
Sir Anthony James Legget (with Alexei A. Abrikosov and Vitaly L. Ginzburg) – 2003

Physiology or Medicine
John James Macleod (with Frederick Grant Banting) – 1923
James Dewey Watson (with Francis Harry Compton Crick and Maurice High Frederick Wilkins) – 1962
Sir James W. Black (with Gertrude B. Elion and George H. Hutchings) – 1988
Barry James Marshall (with J. Robin Warren) – 2005

Peace
Jimmy Carter – 2002

Economics
James E. Meade (with Bertil Ohlin) – 1977
James Tobin – 1981
James M. Buchanan, Jr. – 1986
James A. Mirrlees (with William Vickrey) – 1996
James J. Heckman (with Daniel L. McFadden) – 2000

JAMES AT No. 10

The first James to become Prime Minister was **Arthur James Balfour** (1848-1930) who was in charge for three years and 145 days up to 1905. This Conservative who earned himself the nickname "Bloody Balfour", remained unmarried and was the first PM to own a car.

Labour leader **James Ramsay MacDonald** (1866-1937) is one of the few prime ministers to actually gain power twice, first in 1924 and then again from 1929-1935. He is also famous for being the father of future Cabinet minister Malcolm MacDonald and for appointing the first ever female minister, Margaret Bondfield.

Leonard James Callaghan (1912-2005) was the last Labour Prime Minister (1976-1979) until Tony Blair came to power in 1996. His nicknames were "Big Jim" and "Sunny Jim", and he is thought to be the tallest ever UK Prime Minister standing at 6ft 1in. He was also the longest living former Prime Minister surviving until he was 92, passing away eleven days after the death of his wife Audrey. His daughter Margaret became the leader of the House of Lords in 1998.

KING OF THE RING

There have many men named James who have entered
the old sport of pugilism but none are more famous than
James John Corbett (1866-1933), better known as
Gentleman Jim. His legendary rock-solid stance, and his
autobiography *The Roar of the Crowd*, made him a hit with
fans worldwide. Errol Flynn portrayed him in the biopic of
his life story in 1942, although his own acting career didn't
get past the first round!

Another famous Gentleman Jim, **James Raymond
Lonborg**, started his professional baseball career pitching
for the Boston Red Sox in 1965. He played for a year at
Milwaukee Brewers in 1972 but moved the following year
to Philadelphia Phillies until he ended his playing career in
1979. He now works as a dentist in Hanover, Massachusetts.

Welsh hero **Jimmy Wilde** (1892-1969), known to his
fans as 'The Mighty Atom, became the first ever flyweight
champion defeating Young Zulu Kid in 1916. His pale
complexion and unique punching action made him a
formidable opponent and earned him a second nickname
"the ghost with a hammer in his hand".

At 6ft 3ins. **James Jackson Jeffries** (1875-1953) was an
astonishing boxer who took the impact of many punches
without flinching. He became famous for knocking out his
opponent in a heavyweight championship fight in only 55
seconds. Jackson's endurance and stocky build earned him

the name "the Boilermaker". Legend has it that he could run 100 metres in just over 10 seconds.

Born in 1953, the first heavyweight boxing champion to possess a degree was **James "Bonecrusher" Smith**. His first fight was against James "Broad-Axe" Broad and lasted only four rounds.

Another heavyweight champion was **James "Buster" Douglas** who managed to knock out Mike Tyson on February 11th 1990 to take the title. Tyson, at the time, was at his peak and feared by most of the boxing population for his animalistic style and aggression. This is regarded as one of the greatest upsets in the sport's history.

SCORING JAMES

Any fan of Hammer horror movies will know the name of
James Bernard (1925-2001), a man who composed many
of the studio's finest pieces including *The Curse of Frankenstein*
(1957), *Dracula* (1958), *The Gorgon,* (1964), *The Devil Rides Out*
(1968) and the cross genre classic *The Legend of the 7 Golden
Vampires* (1974). Though he moved away from cinema, one
of his last pieces was a new score for FW Murnau's 1922
classic vampire movie, *Nosferatu* in 1997. Bernard won an
Academy Award in 1952, not for his music but for co-writing
the script for *Seven Days to Noon* with Paul Dehn, his real life
partner. He also attended the same school as Christopher Lee
– Wellington College – but the two never met!

James Dooley, Jim to his friends, may not have composed
scores for the most interesting movies ever to have been
released – an example being *The Hollywood Mom's Mystery*
(2004) – but his latest piece of music will be heard and
appreciated by thousands of people a year. Dooley is the
lucky person who was chosen to write the music for the $40
million experience known as The Simpson's Ride which can
be found at Universal Studios, Florida.

Jim Hedges composed the soundtrack for the hit
computer game *Blood Omen 2: Legacy of Kain*.

Funeral directors everywhere probably despise prolific
composer **James Horner**. He's the person who co-

composed the Celine Dion piece My Heart Will Go On (*Titanic* 1997), a firm favourite with mourners up and down the country. His middle name is Roy, by the way.

Another prolific composer is **James Newton Howard** whose diverse body of work has gained him much respect, if not many awards. Notable pieces include *Flatliners* (1990), *The Fugitive* (1993), *Wyatt Earp* (1994) and *Peter Pan* (2003). He has also scored most of M. Night Shyamalan's movies including *The Sixth Sense* (1999), *Unbreakable* (2000), *Signs* (2002), *The Village* (2004), *The Lady in the Water* (2006) and most recently *The Happening* (2008).

James Last is known in the United Kingdom as a big band leader who released tons of party albums in the 1970s and early 1980s – he had over 50 chart albums during this time – but few would know that he is also a respected and much in demand composer and arranger. Born in Germany in 1929, Hansi Last (his real name) originally wanted to conduct opera but jazz influences changed his career path. He went on to sell over 100 million records in 150 countries, collecting 17 platinum, 11 silver and 206 gold discs.

His work has been used for everything; from selling beauty products to setting the scene of a drama series. **James Rado** is the man who co-wrote the stage sensation, *Hair*!

Australians might not give a XXXX but their famous song Waltzing Matilda is actually Scottish in origin. In 1805 Scottish poet Robert Tannahill wrote the words and in 1818 his friend **James Barr** (1779-1860) wrote some music to accompany it. Popular legend states that Barr's tune could have been based on a piece called Go To The Devil and Shake Yourself.

JAMES MY ARSE! – JAMES IN SITCOMS

Ricky Tomlinson played **Jim Royle** in the ground-breaking comedy series, *The Royle Family* (1998-2008). Jim's on screen wife Barbara was portrayed by Sue Johnston. Both shot to fame in the early 1980s playing Bobby and Sheila Grant in Channel 4's hard-hitting Liverpudlian soap opera *Brookside*. As of March 2009 there have only been 22 episodes of this gritty comedy.

Jim Hacker was the central character of two of the most successful situation comedies to come out of the 1980s; *Yes Minister* and *Yes, Prime Minister*. Starring Paul Eddington as Hacker, the series ran from 1980 until 1988 and was Mrs Thatcher's favourite show. The Iron Lady even played out a sketch with Eddington and co-star Nigel Hawthorn in 1984. Who said she never had a sense of humour?

Citizen James was a Ray Galton and Alan Simpson scripted sitcom (though other writers contributed) that ran from 1960 to 1962 and starred Sid James and Bill Kerr. Tinged with the grit of Hancock, but more upbeat, it ran for 33 episodes with James playing a wide-boy gambler with a long-term fiancée played by Liz Fraser.

One of the forgotten sitcoms of late 1980s starred *Likely Lads* actor **James Bolam**. *Andy Capp* (1988) was a TV version of the classic *Daily Mirror* comic strip. Running for only a single series of six episodes it was devoid of a laughter track and bombed.

Actor **James Dreyfus** made his name in the very un-PC sitcom *Gimme Gimme Gimme* (1999-2001) as Tom Farrell, the gay flat mate of Lynda La Hughes (Kathy Burke). Rude and crude, it was patchy at best. Dreyfus crossed over into mainstream sitcom territory proper when he took over the role of Thermo-Man (originally played by Ardal O'Hanlon) for the sixth season of *My Hero* in 2006.

Though billed as a huge sitcom landmark, *The Peter Principle* was a bit of a damp squib. Starring **Jim Broadbent** in the lead role of bank manager Peter Duffley, it lasted only two seasons from 1995 to 1997. Broadbent made a bigger impact as Del Boy's nemesis, bent copper Roy Slater, in three memorable *Only Fools and Horses* episodes; *May the Force Be with You* (1983), *To Hull and Back* (1985) and *The Class of '62* (1991).

Glum faced actor Geoffrey Palmer is a sitcom legend having appeared in more than his fair share of productions including *Butterflies* (1978-83), *Hot Metal* (1986) and *As Time Goes By* (1992-2005). His most famous role though was as **Jimmy Anderson** in the BBC series *The Fall and Rise of Reginald Perrin* (1976-79). The show had Leonard Rossiter in the lead role and though Rossiter died in 1984 a belated sequel was made in 1996. *The Legacy of Reginald Perrin* starred Palmer and most of the original cast. To take a theme from the original series, it was grot!

Jamesie Cotter is one of the supporting characters from hit Scottish comedy *Rab C. Nesbitt*. Cotter is played by Tony Roper, an actor famous for his comedy roles who hit the big screen in 1973 in the very serious Celtic cult horror movie *The Wicker Man* (1973), in the role of postman.

Hollywood hot-shot **James McAvoy** came to prominence starring in the Manchester pub comedy *Early Doors* for the BBC in 2003. Written by Craig Cash and Phil Mealey, McAvoy played Liam, the boyfriend of Mel (Christine Bottomley).

JAMES...I PRESUME?

Though he's not as famous as he should be, Scotsman **James Bruce** (1730-1794) was the guy who discovered the source of the Blue Nile. A tall man standing 6ft 4ins., he built up a reputation as an accomplished gun handler, horseman – and he could speak eleven different languages. It's also rumoured he could handle himself in a fight! Anyway, he reached Lake Tana, the source, on November 14th, 1770.

Who says lawyers can't lead exciting lives? American legal representative **James Sather Hutchinson** (1867-1959) was the first person to ascend such peaks as North Palisade and Mount Humphreys.

James Clark Ross (1800-1862) was born to be an explorer. He joined the Navy aged only eleven under the wings of his uncle Sir John Ross (1777-1856), a man that would influence his life as well as career. Together they located the North Magnetic Pole in 1831.

Mountain man **James Bridger** (1804-1881), Jim or Old Gabe to his friends, led a colourful life originally making his name as a trapper. He discovered the Great Salt Lake in 1824 but became more famous when he created the course known as Bridger's Pass in 1850, an overland route for the US Postal Service, which runs through the Rockies.

GATHERED TOGETHER IN THE NAME OF JAMES

American televangelists have had a lot of bad press
but there is no denying their ability to stir up religious
opinions.

Jim Bakker was, along with his wife Tammy Faye, a
minister of The Assemblies of God. In 1980 Bakker met
a woman called Jessica Hahn and had, according to the
press 'a one night encounter'. This was kept secret for seven
years and came to light at the same time his wife's drug
dependency was exposed. This was the least of his problems
as the next year he was found guilty of 24 counts of
fraud and conspiracy and sentenced to 45 years in prison.
Released after only five years he is once again preaching to
the masses. His middle name is Orson.

Another preacher laid low by a sex scandal was **Billy
James Hargis** (1925-2004), a 6ft 6ins. right-wing
evangelist who was accused of sleeping with students at
his American Christian College in the mid 1970s. His
famous line on the accusations was, "I was guilty of
sin, but not the sin I was accused of". He did return to
preaching with his work being continued by his son Billy
James Hargis, Jr.

A preacher named **Jim Whittington** was charged in
1992, along with four others, of stealing over $800,000
from a woman called Valerie Lust. He had spent several

years in prison for multiple counts including mail fraud and money laundering. He is not related to the author of this book!

The most famous evangelist has to be **Jimmy Swaggart**. Never one to shy away from speaking his mind, he became unstuck when it was revealed that he had been enjoying the company of "a lady of the night". He famously apologised on air about his sins to his congregation in 1988. It worked for a while but he had to apologise again three years later when he "fell" again. But, as they say, you can't keep a good preacher down and he is once again on the TV preaching the good word.

NEW BALLS, JAMES

American left-handed tennis player **Jimmy Connors** is one of the true legends of the sport. He turned professional in 1972 and soon carved a name for himself as a maverick, but exceptional, player and retained his world number one ranking for 160 weeks during the mid-1970s. Jimbo was a popular face at Wimbledon and earned an impressive scorecard:

Year	Opponent	W/RU	Scorecard
1974	Ken Rosewall	W	6-1, 6-1, 6-4
1975	Arthur Ashe	L	6-1, 6-1, 5-7, 6-4
1977	Bjorn Borg	L	3-6, 6-2, 6-1, 5-7, 6-4
1978	Bjorn Borg	L	6-2, 6-2, 6-3
1982	John McEnroe	W	3-6, 6-3, 6-7, 7-6, 6-4
1984	John McEnroe	L	6-1, 6-1, 6-2

He is also one of the few players to win a championship on all three tennis surfaces; grass, clay and hard.

Jim Courier (middle name Spencer) is not only a former American and world number one player, but is also a successful businessman with his event company, InsideOut Sports & Entertainment. He reached the Wimbledon final in 1993 but was beaten by Pete Sampras 7-6, 7-6, 3-6, 6-3. He was inducted into the International Tennis Hall of Fame in 2005.

Another American not to bag a Wimbledon title is **Jim Grabb**, although his career as a doubles player has been exceptional. He has won 23 Grand Slam doubles titles and a notable singles win against Andre Agassi (1-6, 6-4, 6-2) in South Korea in 1987. Jim's 6ft 4ins. frame no doubt helps him with lob shots.

Though not really known in the United Kingdom, American base-line player **Jimmy Arias** had an incredible start to his career. A gifted and natural player, he became the youngest player to achieve a world ranking, aged just 15, and turned professional a year later. A mentally strong player, he only won five tournaments (all on clay) during his career.

A player who overcame physical problems to achieve great things is **James Blake**. He took up tennis at only five years of age but when he turned 13 doctors diagnosed him with severe scoliosis (curvature of the spine) and he had to wear a full back brace for up to 18 hours every day. He recovered enough to begin a tennis career in 1999. James was to suffer more heartache in 2004 when he broke his neck on a clay court and also contracted shingles. Further tragedy followed that year when his father died of stomach cancer. Once more James pushed himself to return to the professional circuit at the end of 2005. He has set up the Thomas Blake Sr. Memorial Research Fund in memory of his father.

Ventriloquist James

Multi talented performer **Jim Barber** is best known for his routine "Jim Barber and Seville", a piece where it looks as if he and another puppet (named Diva) are actually being operated and held by another puppet named Seville, who stands six feet tall! A noted mimic and vocal contortionist, he is a huge hit wherever he plays. He is not to be confused with another **Jim Barber**, the motivational speaker who has produced a book entitled *Quit Fondling the Elephant's Ass*. It is designed to encourage people to view problems from different perspectives! Both are not to be confused with businessman **Jim Barber** who once dated Courtney Love!

Back to James in the studio

Chris James is a Birmingham-based newsreader and journalist who presents the award-winning *Central News* for the ITV Network.

On September 11th 2001, one of the BBC's lead reporters for the Twin Towers disaster was **James Robbins**. He also covered the release of Nelson Mandela and was one of the first journalists to interview him after his incarceration.

Jim Muir has been the BBC's Middle East correspondent since 1995. He is best known for his coverage of some of the biggest news stories in recent years including the Gulf War.

Though famous for his entertainment report show *E24* for BBC News, **James Dagwell** has been a reporter for *Newsround* and a presenter/reporter for ITV1 West Country. According to the BBC he got his big break as a tea-boy at GMTV.

Journalist and TV presenter **James May** began his career as a writer but is more famous for his work on the TV series *Top Gear*. In 1992, he was fired from *Autocar Magazine* for putting a secret, and rather cheeky, message into the magazine's Road Test Year Book supplement. It took him two attempts to pass his driving test.

SCRIPTING JAMES

An accomplished playwright, **Jim Beaver** is famous for
playing Whitney Ellsworth in the hit HBO series *Deadwood*.
Jim wrote three plays for Actors Theatre of Louisville at
the end of the 1970s and continued to pen original works
including scripts for *Alfred Hitchcock Presents* until the writers'
strike of 1988. He has been working on a project about
tragic Superman actor George Reeves that he hopes to
develop for the screen.

Due to the coincidence of two leading actors in the
Superman role both dying tragically – George Reeves
committed suicide in 1959, aged 45, and Christopher Reeve
was paralysed after a riding accident in 1995 and died in
2004, aged 52 – rumours of a curse connected with the
Man of Steel character has become part of cinema history.

Colorado Tolston is the pseudonym of American playwright
T. James Belich. He lists C.S. Lewis as one of his major
influences and has created over a dozen plays which vary in
genre from murder mystery and science fiction to children's
fantasy and folk stories.

Another James who relied on a pseudonym was Scottish
playwright Osborne Henry Mavor (1888-1951). Writing as
James Bridie his most famous work was on three movies
with Alfred Hitchcock; *The Paradine Case* (1947), *Under
Capricorn* (1949) and *Stage Fright* (1950) but he also wrote
many comedies, albeit with dark undertones, and several

BBC plays were adapted from his stage work including *Mr. Gillie* (1957) and *Jonah and the Whale* (1950). He studied medicine at the University of Glasgow (he was a military doctor) where the Glasgow University Union Library has been named after his alias.

Born in Liverpool in 1949, **Jimmy McGovern** has become one of the most respected TV writers in the country. His work on Phil Redmond's *Brookside* for Channel 4 gave him the experience to write gritty and realistic drama culminating in *Hillsborough* in 1996, a dramatised play based around the football stadium disaster. Jimmy has also given us one of TV's most enduring characters when he created *Cracker*, with Robbie Coltrane in the lead role of criminal psychologist Dr. Edward "Fitz" Fitzgerald. The series was recreated for American audiences in 1997 with Robert Pastorelli stepping into Coltrane's shoes.

OLYMPIC JAMES

On April 6th, 1896 the first modern Olympic Games were held in Athens, Greece. On that very same day the first gold medal was won by American triple jumper **James Connolly** (this was the original two hops and a skip version), which classes him as the first ever champion of the modern Olympics. At the same tournament he won silver in the high jump and bronze in the long jump. He would compete in the Paris Olympics of 1900 but only managed to get silver in the triple jump this time around.

American competitor **Jim Thorpe** proved that he was world class in Stockholm 1912, winning gold in the pentathlon and decathlon events. His achievement was tarnished when it was revealed that he had been paid to play minor-league baseball. The Olympic rules at the time stipulated that all athletes had to be amateur and his name was removed from the Roll of Champions. Thorpe's family had to wait until 1982 for the Olympic Committee to reverse their decision. Unfortunately, Jim didn't live to see it as he passed away in 1953.

Equestrian rider **Mark James Todd** has two Olympic gold medals to his name; one at Los Angeles in 1984 and one at Seoul in 1988 – both achieved on his horse Charisma. At the team event in 1988 he bagged a bronze and would also get a third place at the 2000 Olympics in Sydney. That was on the horse Eyespy II. Charisma broke his shoulder, aged 30, and didn't survive.

British swimmer **Andrew Jameson** won bronze in the 1988 Seoul Olympics, in the 100m butterfly event. He now commentates on the sport for the BBC. His sister Helen won silver in the Olympics of 1980 in the 4 x 100m relay.

Jim Shea, Jr. comes from a family of American Olympic sportsmen. His grandfather, Jack, won two gold medals in the 1932 Olympics for speed skating. Jim Sr. participated in the Innsbruck Olympics of 1964 but failed to make the podium. Jim Jr. on the other hand won gold in Salt Lake City 2002 in the bobsleigh event. Tragically, just 17 days before the opening ceremony, Jim's grandfather was killed by a drunk driver. To spur himself on Jim Jr. placed a picture of his grandfather in his crash helmet.

Hilda May James competed in the Belgium Olympics of 1920 bagging a silver medal as part of the women's 4 x 100m freestyle relay team along with Constance Jeans, Charlotte Radcliff and Grace McKenzie. James also competed in the women's 300m freestyle but finished fourth.

Scottish-born bronze medallist **James Harper-Orr** stood on the podium at the 1908 London Olympics with the rest of the men's hockey team.

Team GB had their best medals win in over a century during the 2008 Beijing Olympics, bagging 19 gold, 13 silver and 15 bronze medals. In the London Olympics in

1908 Team GB won 56 gold medals. Team GB did even better in the 2008 Paralympics by collecting 42 gold, 29 silver and 31 bronze medals – their best performance in twenty years – second only to China.

Jameses that struck gold in 2008:

Rowing – men's coxless: **Tom James**, Steve Williams, Pete Reed and Andy Hodge

Boxing – middleweight: **James DeGale**

Swimming – men's 200m S2 freestyle and S2 50m backstroke: **Jim Anderson** won the silver medal as well as grabbing a bronze in the men's S2 100m freestyle

S2 forms part of a classification table that is used to help group disabled athletes into an order so they compete with others of similar abilities for the swimming events. S1 ranks as severely disabled whilst S10 is minimally disabled.

———⬗◆⬖———

KING OF THE RING – 2!

Duncan Airlie James was the first Scotsman to become a world champion in kick boxing and Thai boxing. Along with Kevin Maguire, he set up Battle Group International in 2001 – a promoter of international fights – when he retired from the sport. One of their aims is to give events a more family-friendly atmosphere.

With a tag-line that reads "Sorry about your damn luck" wrestler **Cowboy James Storm** (born James Allan Black) is a force in the ring. His original dream of being a basketball player was scuppered by a shoulder injury.

HEAVENLY BODIES, JAMES

Astronomer Royal **James Bradley** (1693-1762) is credited with discovering the aberration of light (an astronomical occurrence that produces an apparent motion of celestial objects) but this was a bit of serendipitous luck as he was actually researching the stellar parallax (the disparity in bearing of a celestial object as seen by a viewer from two broadly separated points)! His uncle was another noted astronomer, **Rev. James Pound**.

On June 22nd 1978 **James W. Christie**, along with Robert S. Harrington, discovered Charon, the largest moon that orbits the planet Pluto. The name Charon – he transported the souls of the dead across the river Styx – comes from Greek mythology. The asteroid 129564 Christy was named after him.

James Clark Maxwell (1831-1879) was the first astronomer to theoretically suggest (in his paper on "The stability of the motion of Saturn's rings, 1859") that Saturn's rings were formed from orbiting debris and not solid as it was thought of at the time. People had to wait until 1895 when **James Edward Keeler** (1857-1900), using spectroscopic technology, confirmed Maxwell's theory.

The asteroid 3594 Scotti is named after American **James Vernon Scotti**, an astronomer who has discovered numerous comets and asteroids.

DOCTOR JAMES

British paediatrician **James Mourilyan Tanner**
invented the Tanner Stages, scales for sexual development
in puberty. There are five stages in the three different
sections, one each for male and female and a combined
one for both sexes.

Sir James Paget (1814-1899) has the honour of
having many different diseases named after him. Paget's
abscess is an abscess that returns to the place where
a different abscess had once occupied and was cured.
Paget's disease is a deformity of the bones also known as
Osteitis Deformans. Extramammary Paget disease is an
uncommon cancer.

Probably one of the most famous diseases to be named
after a person is Parkinson's disease. **James Parkinson**
(1755-1824) was the first person to investigate shaking
palsy (paralysis agitans) in 1817. Sixty years later French
neurologist Jean-Martin Charcot was the person who
actually adapted the name Parkinson's disease to the
syndrome after his own research.

James Manby Gully MD (1808-83) developed the
hydrotherapy process which he perfected with **Dr. James
Wilson**. Gully's achievement is overshadowed by the fact
that he was once a suspect in the Charles Bravo poisoning
case. Bravo was the new love interest of Florence Ricardo, a

woman who Gully had once had a brief fling with. Jealousy was the cited motive but Gully was cleared of any doing with the case.

REALLY A JAMES

James Roderick Moir is the real name of surreal comedian and singer Vic Reeves. Legend has it he formed the name from singers Vic Damone and Jim Reeves. In 1991 Vic teamed up with the Wonder Stuff to record the number one hit Dizzy (a cover of the Tommy Roe track from 1969) and then hit number three in 1995 when he and comedy partner Bob Mortimer teamed up with EMF to cover The Monkees hit I'm a Believer. The lead singer of EMF was **James Atkin**.

Dashing movie star Stewart Granger (1913-93) won many female hearts but few would have known that his real name was **James Leblanche Stewart.**

The plastic man of punk Iggy Pop was actually born **James Newell Osterberg**. Known for his explosive stage performances and his excessive drug taking, he found the time to star in the Nickelodeon family comedy *Snow Day* (2000) alongside Chevy Chase.

Do They Know It's Christmas co-composer Midge Ure OBE was born **James Ure** on October 10th, 1953. Famous for fronting 1980s electronic music pioneers Ultravox, whilst sporting a penile thin moustache, he went on to enjoy a successful solo career notching up six top 40 hits. His daughter Molly is also carving herself a career in the music industry. Midge is actually a reversal of his name;

start with James, shorten to Jim, then reverse it to become Mij. Midge is the phonetic version of Mij. See, easy!

Lauren Charlotte Harries was born **James Charles Harries** in 1978. He/she shot to fame after appearing on *Wogan*, aged 12. Dressed in shirt and tie and sporting a mop of blonde curly hair that Harpo Marx would have been proud of, the youngster proclaimed to be an antiques expert and boasted about being able to spot bargains at car boot fairs. His media pull waned as he grew into a teenager and in 2001, Harries underwent sex reassignment surgery.

A COMPLETELY RANDOM JAMES

In Tokyo on a week's holiday James McMullan blagged a backstage pass after an Ian Brown concert and went for dinner with the band. Walking drunkenly through the entertainment district Shinjuku, Ian Brown and James both took three minute turns sparring with a late-night street boxer. They didn't hit him once.

JAMES IN THE MIDDLE

Gangsta rapper 50 Cent has had quite a controversial career. Do you think he would have made the same angry impact if he'd used his real name of **Curtis James Jackson III?**

Regularly voted as one of the greatest actors of all time, **Alfredo James Pacino** – Al to his friends – has surprisingly only ever won one Academy Award, and that was for *Scent of a Woman* (1992). He has been nominated seven times.

Heavy Metal vocalist and multi-instrumentalist **Ronnie James Dio** has performed in many bands including Elf, Rainbow and Black Sabbath. His real Christian name is Padavona but he changed it to Dio as it means 'God' in Italian.

One of America's greatest sons was football player and actor, **Orenthal James Simpson** (O. J. or the Juice to his friends). But all of his achievements on the pitch and on big screen have been overshadowed by a real life tragedy. O. J.'s ex-wife Nicole Brown Simpson and her friend Ronald Goldman were found murdered in her home on June 12th, 1994. O. J. became number one suspect and his escape from the police in his white 4x4 was shown live on US TV. O. J. was found not guilty on October 3rd, 1995 but the tragic events have seen his career continually slide ever since.

FAILING JAMES

Astronomer **Professor James Challis** (1803-82) has a notable failure to his name… He missed the chance of discovering the planet Neptune in 1846! He put it down to the amount of comets he was studying at the time.

King George III was almost assassinated on May 15th 1800 by **James Hadfield**, who fired a shot at the monarch whilst at the Theatre Royal, Drury Lane. He was acquitted when sent to trial as he was considered to be insane.

JAMES THROUGH HOOPS

Canadian physical education instructor **James A. Naismith** invented the sport of basketball in 1891. He died in 1939 but twenty years later the Naismith Basketball Hall of Fame was established.

Basketball star **LeBron James** is often compared to Michael Jordan not only because he is a fine player but because he wears the same shirt numbers. At the 2004 Olympics James wore number 9 and Jordan wore that number at the 1984 and 1992 games. In normal matches James wears 23, as did Jordan.

Tragically, Michael Jordan's father James was killed whilst taking a break from driving in 1993.

James Gist is a 6ft 9ins. player who has plenty to do on and off the court. Apart from playing for the Maryland college team, he volunteered to help at the Special Olympics and work in soup kitchens.

THE JAMES PART IS RIGHT

Hollywood heart-throb **James Garner** was actually christened James Scott Baumgarner when he was born on April 7th, 1928. A naturally gifted actor, he appeared in many of Hollywood's most memorable movies such as *Move Over Darling* (1963), *The Great Escape* (1963) and *Support Your Local Sheriff* (1969). Television also played a major part in his life: in 1957 he portrayed cowboy *Maverick* and turned detective as Jim Rockford in *The Rockford Files* in 1974. Garner received a Purple Heart after being wounded during the Korean War.

Famous for putting his arms up the back of cattle in the Yorkshire Dales, veterinarian turned novel writer James Herriot was actually born **James Alfred Wright** (1916-1995) in Sunderland.

With a singing career spanning over fifty years, **Etta James** (born Jamesetta Hawkins in 1938) is one of the most famous and powerful singers to come out of the 20th century. It is said that even at the age of five she could command an audience when she sang in church. Her adult life – she became a drug addict and often dated violent men – is as colourful as her vocal range.

OCH AYE THE JAMES!

Scottish poet **James Hogg** (1770-1835) had to wait until 1807 before his work would get the acknowledgment that it deserved. *The Mountain Bard* was his first hit but in 1813 his book, *The Queen's Wake*, a piece about Queen Mary, was the one that catapulted him at the top of the Scottish literary scene.

Naughty **James Hepburn** (1536-1578) was the 4th Earl of Bothwell, as well as being the Lord High Admiral of Scotland. He led a colourful life. Apart from being the third husband of Mary Queen of Scots, he had an eye for adventure as well as the ladies. He courted many noble women, including Anna Rustung; married Lady Jean Gordon, then divorced her, and ended up marrying the aforementioned Queen on May 15th, 1567. Not surprisingly, he died at the young age of 44.

Noted farmer **James Hutton** (1726-1797) is considered by many to be the founder of modern geology. Originally a student of chemistry, he began to work on a farm that was handed down from his family to him. It was here his fascination with rocks and their formation was sparked and after extensive research he discovered that the heat from deep inside the Earth caused these formations and that the surface of the planet continually refreshed itself. Thus he went on to to state that the Earth was far older than previously thought – being millions of years old instead of just 6,000 – a common thought at the time. His paper, *Theory of the Earth* was published in 1788.

Woman around the globe have Glaswegian **Sir James Young Simpson** (1811-1870) to thank for his pioneering use of chloroform to help ease the pain experienced during childbirth. Not taken seriously at first, his work became respected after Queen Victoria used it during the birth of Prince Leopold. He has another first to his name; he was the first person to be knighted for his services to medicine.

The most famous Scotsman to make a mark during the Industrial Revolution was **James Watt** (1736-1819); his modifications (and not the invention) of the steam engine made him a wealthy man. Few know that he termed the scientific word "horsepower" whereas everyone probably knows the unit of electricity – the Watt – is named in his honour.

JAMES IN THE SONG

Avant-garde singer-songwriter Kate Bush released her first album, The Kick Inside, on February 17th 1978. Apart from the hit singles Wuthering Heights (her only UK number one) and The Man With The Child In His Eyes, you'll also find a track called **James & The Cold Gun**. It's track 7, if you want to skip straight to it.

Louis Armstrong was one of the first performers of the now classic, **St. James Infirmary Blues**. Since he laid down his version in 1928 literally hundreds of artists have taken stabs at it including The Animals, Janis Joplin, The Triffids, Tom Jones and The White Stripes. Written by Irvin Mills (writing as Joe Primrose) it's a sad song containing many blues clichés.

American hip-hop survivors the Beastie Boys (apparently, the name stands for **B**oys **E**ntering **A**narchistic **S**tates **T**owards **I**nternal **E**xcellence) originally formed in 1981 with members Adam Yuach and Mike Diamond. Two other musicians, John Berry and Kate Schellenbach, were also part of the team at this time. After a short split they reformed this time with Adam Horovitz and a legend was born, sort of. **Jimmy James** is the first track on their 1992 release Check Your Head.

Not so vain singer-songwriter Carly Simon composed the song **James** for her 1980 album Come Upstairs. James

Taylor was her husband at the time and he performs backing vocals on three tracks; Stardust, Them and Jesse.

Independent group Pop Will Eat Itself – who had minor hits with Love Missile F1-11 and Can U Dig It – recorded the single **Not Now James, We're Busy** in 1989.

Right-on singer-songwriter Billy Bragg released the album William Bloke in September 1996 featuring the track **King James Version**.

Eccentric pop duet They Might Be Giants scored their biggest UK hit in 1990 with the track Birdhouse In Your Soul. They wrote the track **James K. Polk**, about the eleventh US President, for the album Factory Showroom (1996). They also sang the song **Meet James Ensor**, about the famous Belgian painter, for the album John Henry (1994).

Scientist **James Burke** is name-checked in the track The Black Hit of Space by Human League. It features on the 1980 album Travelogue.

Jimmy Jimmy was a track on the first album from The Undertones (1979). The eponymous collection of songs from the Northern Irish band was not their first release; an earlier EP contained the single Teenage Kicks (originally released in 1978) and was championed by DJ John Peel, becoming his favourite record of all time.

Martha Reeves and the Vandellas had a handful of hits in the British charts during the 1960s, most of them on the Motown label. Jimmy Mack reached number 21 in 1967, and reached the same position when it was re-released in 1970.

CORONATION STREET JAMES

Coronation Street is the country's longest running, and perhaps most popular, soap opera. It all started on December 9th 1960 and was created by Tony Warren. Set in Manchester, it began as a realistically shot series, focusing on the class struggles of the era. Originally planned as a 13-part series, it has gone on to form the backbone of the ITV schedule. The soap has transformed over the years and although it is still set in the same area, the social commentary has been replaced by sensationalist drama.

Perpetual loser **Jim McDonald** has been in and out of the soap for nearly 20 years. The fiery character, played by Charles Lawson, has been married to Liz (Beverly Callard) twice and killed gangster Jez Quigley (Lee Boardman) in September 2000.

He has twin boys, Steve and Andy, and tragedy struck in 1992 when daughter Katie died only a few hours old.

In the mid-1970s there were two children who played havoc with the residents of Coronation Street. **Jimmy Haggerty** and his brother Kevin harangued the residents with their wild and naughty pranks.

Alma Halliwell's first husband was **Jim Sedgwick** (Michael O'Hagan). Their relationship was a total disaster and culminated in her getting an abortion. They divorced and he left, leaving Alma to find love with Mike Baldwin (Johnny Briggs). Alma, played by Amanda Barrie, died of cervical cancer in 2001. She made a name for herself in the movie *Carry On...Cleo* (1964), in the lead role.

Barrie and Briggs reached the UK pop charts in 1995 with a cover version of the Frank and Nancy Sinatra classic Something Stupid. Its highest position was 35.

Nick Conway shot to fame in Carla Lane's Liverpudlian comedy *Bread* in 1986. Typecast by his role as hapless Billy he's been rarely seen on TV since. He popped up in Coronation Street as **Mr. Jameson** in 1997, Liz McDonald's boss at the Warwick Hotel Bar.

Rita Fairclough (Barbara Knox) has had her fair share of partners. Before she was married to Len Fairclough she had a brief fling with married man **Jimmy Graham** (Colin George). Needless to say, it ended in tears. Rita had another run in with a James, this time in 2002, when would-be robber **Johnny James** (William Ash) hi-jacked her car. He got more than he bargained for as the other occupants were Betty, Blanche and Emily!

Perpetual ladies man Devendra Alahan first walked the cobbled streets in November of 1999. Played by **Jimmi Harkishin**, Dev has had many women swoon after him but has also enjoyed embarrassing moments. His one-night fling with Deirdre Barlow in 2001 is regularly voted as one of the most cringe-worthy pieces of TV ever. Though the event was kept a secret from her family for a time, it all came out when Dev started dating Deirdre's daughter, Tracey. What a guy! Harkishin was born in Paris, France in 1965 to Indian and Italian parents.

THE FIRST JAMES TO...

Legendary science fiction author **Forrest James Ackerman** – Acker-Man to his friends – was one of the first people to approach J.R.R. Tolkien to make an animated version of *The Lord of the Rings*. Tolkien turned him down. Ackerman is best known for coining the term 'Sci-Fi' and creating the cult magazine *Famous Monsters of Filmland* (1958-1983).

The steam hammer was invented by Scotsman **James Hall Nasmyth** in 1839.

James Dyson cleaned up when he invented the world's first dual cyclone and bagless vacuum cleaner. Prior to this, he designed the ballbarrow, a design he would return to and adapt for his vacuum cleaners making them easier to clean around corners.

Sheffield-born **James Stuart Blackton** (1875-1941) holds his place in history as being the inventor of Stop Motion Film technique.

Jacques-Yves Cousteau (1910-1997) was not only a respected ecologist and filmmaker but also co-developed the aqualung and the world's first underwater television camera which led to Jacques filming the first ever undersea footage in colour from 1952–1953.

American inventor **James Leonard Plimpton** designed the world's first controllable roller skates, known as rocker skates, in 1863. His design was an improvement on the inline skates which were originally designed by John Joseph Merlin in 1760 but could not be guided.

Smokers may like to thank (or may not as the case may be) **James Albert Bonsack** (1859-1924) who patented the first ever cigarette rolling machine way back in 1881. This steam powered piece of machinery could produce thousands in a day and made smoking cheaper for everyone.

One of the founding members of the Order of the Garter was **Sir James Audley** (1316-1386).

The first dry wholegrain cereal – Granula – was invented by **Dr James Caleb Jackson** (1811-1895). This tasty sounding snack was composed of dense bran nuggets that were soaked to make them chewable and easier to swallow.

Though it sounds like a plot from a pulp/cyberpunk crossover novel, the first person to be convicted of an Internet related murder was **James D. Pritchert**. His wife, Lila, was spending a lot of time online "talking" to friends in a chat room and on the night of November 7th 1995 he spoke to her about it. It was at this time she announced she wanted a divorce. After arguing, Pritchert suffocated Lila using a pillow. He confessed to the crime and was sentenced to 11 years.

In 2003 **James Gibson** became the first Briton in 28 years to win a world title in the 50m breaststroke long course class. The multiple medal winner was honoured with an MBE in 2004.

JAMES IN DOCTOR WHO

Jimmy Vee is an actor who specialises in playing many of the smaller creations for the regenerated series of *Doctor Who*. He was The Moxx of Ballhoon (*The End of the World* 2005), a Space Pig (*Aliens of London* 2005) and Bannakaffalatta (*Voyage of the Damned* 2007). Jimmy also appeared in an online game for the show as the lead character in *Attack of the Graske*.

Writer **James Moran** penned the story *Fires of Pompeii* (2008) and also an episode of the *Doctor Who* spin-off series *Torchwood*; *Sleeper* (2008).

Seventh Doctor Sylvester McCoy was actually born **Percy James Patrick Kent-Smith**. A gifted stage performer, he began his career as part of the Ken Campbell Roadshow where he would hammer six inch nails up his nose. McCoy played the Doctor from 1987 to 1989, when the show was eventually cancelled. Some argue that because he appeared in the Children in Need skit *Dimension in Time* (1993), and starred in the *TV Movie* (1996) where Paul McGann became the eight Doctor, his tenure as the noble Time Lord was actually one of the longest!

Liver Bird **Polly James** popped up in the Peter Davison two-part story *The Visitation* in 1984.

James Muir is a character actor who not only appeared in *Doctor Who* on many occasions but also landed roles in BBC classics such as *The Goodies* (1977), *The Hitch-Hikers Guide to the Galaxy* (1981) and *Blake's 7* (1980 and 1981).

To keep some characters' appearances secret, *Radio Times* often uses pseudonyms to help keep certain pieces of the plot away from the public. One of the most famous instances was to credit **James Stoker** in the role of Sir Gilles in the 1983 two-part story *The King's Demons*. James Stoker is an anagram of Masters Joke and was actually played by Anthony Ainley in his most famous role – The Master.

James Robert McCrimmon, or Jamie to his friends, was one of the longest serving companions the good Doctor had. Played by Frazer Hines, this highlander was often left bemused by the technology used by the Doctor. Hamish Wilson played Jamie in episodes two and three of *The Mind Robber* (1968) as Hines was poorly at the time of recording. Frazer also played another well-loved TV character; Joe Sugden on *Emmerdale Farm* – which changed to just *Emmerdale* – from 1972 to 1994, though Joe wasn't killed off until 1995.

Award-winning television director **James Hawes** has been behind some of the revamped show's most memorable moments. He directed the Hugo Award-winning episodes *The Empty Child* and *The Doctor Dances*, both shown in 2005, and *The Christmas Invasion* also shown that year. He also directed the return of Sarah Jane Smith in the 2006 episodes; *School Reunion* and *New Earth*.

JAMES IN THE GRANDSTAND

With a chin that would make Bruce Forsyth jealous, **Jimmy Hill** is one of the most famous presenters and football pundits to have appeared on our screens. His colourful career began in 1949 as a footballer, first at Brentford before moving to Fulham in 1953. He became manager of Coventry City in 1961 and took the Sky Blues from Division Three to the top flight but is more famous for being a football expert, as well as a broadcaster. He fronted *Match of the Day* on and off from 1973 to 1988, and was succeeded by silky smooth Des Lynam.

Belfast-born commentator **Jim Neilly** took over BBC boxing commentating duties from the legendary Harry Carpenter. Jim was originally a science teacher.

Formula 1 commentator **James Allen** has moved into the seat once occupied by the great Murray Walker. He has covered over 100 races for ITV as well as publishing several noted books on the sport.

One of the most famous radio sports voices belongs to announcer **James Alexander Gordon**. James suffered from polio as a child, at one point causing paralysis. He began to practice reading the football scores, aged eight, to his adoptive father to help ease a speech impediment that he suffered from. James has read the football results on the BBC's *Sports Report* for over 30 years.

JAMES OF LONDON

The position of The Lord Mayor of the City of London was created in 1189 and the person elected is in the position for a year, running from November to November. The job is to act as an Ambassador for the UK and is not to be confused with The Mayor of London title, which was created in 2000. James has featured prominently over the years:

James Alderman	1216
James Andreu	1367
Sir Bartholomew James	1479
James Yarford	1519
James Spencer	1527
James Hawes	1574
James Harvye	1581
Sir James Pemberton	1611
Sir James Campbell	1629
Sir James Edwards	1678
Sir James Smyth	1684
Sir James Bateman	1716
James Townshend	1772
Sir James Sanderson	1792
Sir James Duke	1848
James Whitehead	1888
Sir James Ritchie	1903
James Roll	1920
Sir James Harman	1963
Sir James Miller	1964

POETIC JAMES

James Thompson (1700-1748) wrote many pieces of classic poetry including the four-part epic, *The Seasons*, which was released as *Winter* (1726), *Summer* (1727), *Spring* (1728) and *Autumn* (1730). In 1740 Thompson wrote the masque, *Alfred the Great* which contained the lyrics of Rule Britannia. Thomas Arne set it to music.

Poet and civil rights activist **James Weldon Johnson** (1871-1938) composed *Lift Ev'ry Voice and Sing* between 1899 and 1900, a piece that was originally written to celebrate Abraham Lincoln's birthday (February 12th) but was taken to heart by African Americans and became known as The Negro National Hymn.

Kiwi poet **James K. Baxter** (1926-1972) was known to some as Hemi and had the middle name Keir. This was given to him by his parents, who favoured the left side for their politics in respect for Keir Hardie.

James Oppenheim (1882-1932) was a poet who reflected the industrial movement and hard times of the early 20th century in his prose. His most famous quote is: "The foolish man seeks happiness in the distance; the wise grows it under his feet". He also helped to set up literary magazine *The Seven Arts*.

Often referred to as The Bard of Ballycarry, **James Orr** (1770-1816) was usually classed as a Weaver poet, a name given to working class poets from Ulster around the time he died.

>•<

JAMES THE CHEF

North Yorkshire-born **James Masters** (b. 1972) is a celebrity chef who gets his passion for cookery from his father who was manager of the catering services at Castle Howard. Rumour has it that James actually cooked for the Queen Mother when he was just 12 years of age.

Four years later he was training at Scarborough Technical College where, for three years running, he was awarded Student of the Year. He was spotted by Antony Worrall Thompson and the rest, as they say, is culinary history.

Described by *Time* as 'The Food Oscars', **The James Beard Foundation Awards** were established in 1990 and were designed to highlight the finest of the food and beverage industry in America. James Beard (1903-1985) himself was one of the first ever TV chefs, starting in 1946 with his ground-breaking series paving the way for countless imitators. He also started his own cookery school, wrote seminal books on food and championed local produce inspiring America to recognise its culinary heritage.

Jamie Oliver (born James Trevor Oliver in 1975) was, like many chefs, influenced by his parents. His father runs The Cricketers pub in Essex and young Jamie was allowed to help out. This sparked his interest in creating dishes. His campaign for healthy school meals earned him an MBE and his TV shows have won many awards. Jamie's musical career wasn't as pukka as his catering one. His group Scarlet Division was dropped after they failed to impress the record buying public.

Dr James Salisbury (1823-1905) is classed as one of the earliest health food practitioners, a sort of Gillian McKeith of his time. He was one of the first to design special diets for his patients and went on to create The Salisbury Steak, which was simply lean beef that had all of its muscle and connective tissue removed and was then mashed, shaped then broiled. It was then seasoned to taste. Nice!

ONE-OFF JAMES

If you used the name **James** in a game of Scrabble then you would earn 14 points. J = 8, A = 1, M = 3, E = 1 and S = 1.

There is a species of flamingo called **James's Flamingo**, named after Harry Berkely James. It is also known as Puna Flamingo (Phoenicopterus jamesi).

Blu Peter, a male DJ who hit the charts in 1998 for one week with the single Tell Me What You Want/**James Has Kittens**. It reached number 70. It was his only chart entry.

A true one-off is the Angry Video Game Nerd, a comedy character created by **James D. Rolfe**. The Nerd reviews retro games online and his video posts have gained a cult following.

The Fan Man, aka **James Jarrett Miller** (1963-2002), was someone who would paraglide and crash (literally) into famous sporting events or places. His most outrageous gate-crashing stunt was also his first, at the Evander Holyfield versus Riddick Bowe fight at Caesars Palace in 1993. The crowd attacked him after he hit the ring and he was beaten unconscious. In 1994 he landed on top of Buckingham Palace daubed in green paint, with his testicles painted day-glo. He disappeared in 2002 and was found hanging from a tree in 2003. Verdict was suicide.

The official number one GI Joe fan in the world is **James DeSimone**. He was given the title by manufacturer Hasbro who gave him a handmade GI Joe which bared his likeness. His collection of merchandise goes back to 1964, the year when the toy was released, and covers the entire range.

James Montgomery Flagg (1877-1960) recreated one of the most iconic images ever committed to paper. His drawing of Uncle Sam pointing at the reader with the legend "I Want You for the US Army" was designed for the World War I effort. Drawn up for a poster in 1917, it was actually an American version of a British idea. In 1914 Lord Kitchener was Secretary of State for War and a poster with Kitchener pointing at the reader with the words "Your Country Needs You" below his image was designed to help encourage people to enlist. It was created by Alfred Leete.

THERE'S LIFE JIM, BUT NOT AS WE KNOW IT

Star Trek is one of the most famous TV and movie franchises
to have come out of the US. The most famous character
was **Captain James Tiberius Kirk**, played to high camp,
pantomime perfection by William Shatner. Kirk was a man's
man, a brave hero with an eye for the ladies and a hand
always on his weapon. His middle name of Tiberius comes
from the Roman Emperor Tiberius Caesar Augustus. The
character had one son, David Marcus, who was tragically
killed in the movie *Star Trek II: Wrath of Khan* (1982).

Shatner himself has led a varied career, not only starring
in the TV hits *T.J. Hooker* (1982-1985) and *Boston Legal*,
but he has made many acclaimed cameos. He was the Big
Giant Head character in the comedy series *Third Rock from
the Sun*, and ridiculed Star Trek fans on *Saturday Night Live*.
He has also enjoyed a recording career releasing "original"
versions of such classics as Lucy in the Sky With Diamonds
and Mr. Tambourine Man, both from his 1968 album
The Transformed Man. He also attempted to cover Pulp's
Common People for his 2004 album Has Been.

Actor, director, singer and star of the classic TV series *Time Tunnel*
(1966-1967), **James Darren** also popped up on *Star Trek: Deep
Space 9* (1993-1999). In this the second spin off from *Star Trek* –
not counting *Star Trek – The Animated Series* which ran from 1973-
1974 – Darren played Vic Fontaine, an all-singing smart-alec
hologram who became quite a hit with fans for some reason.

Doctor James Moriarty (as played by Daniel Davis)
appeared in the *Star Trek: The Next Generation* episode
Elementary, Dear Data in 1988.

James Horan has appeared in a number of *Star Trek*
episodes as various characters:

Star Trek: The Next Generation:
- Dr Jo 'Brill – *Suspicious* (1993)
- Lieutenant Barnaby – *Descent Part 2* (1993)

Star Trek: Deep Space 9:
- Ikat'ika – *In Purgatory's Shadow* (1997)
- Ikat'ika – *By Inferno's Light* (1997)

Star Trek: Voyager:
- Tosin – *Fair Trade* (1997)

Star Trek: Enterprise:
- Humanoid Figure – *Broken Bow Parts 1 and 2* (2001)
- Humanoid Figure – *Shockwave Parts 1 and 2* (2002)
- Humanoid Figure – *The Expanse* (2003)

He has also loaned his voice to a couple of *Star Trek* video games:

Star Trek: Klingon Academy (2000)
Star Trek: Starfleet Command (2002)

JAMES THE PLACE

There are scores of places with James in the name.

Here's a handful:

Baldersby St. James	Yorkshire
Chignall St. James	Essex
Sutton St. James	Lincolnshire
St. James	Dorset
St. James's End	Northamptonshire
St. James South Elmham	Suffolk
James City	Pennsylvania, USA
Jamestown	New York, USA
Jameson	Missouri, USA
James Craik	Argentina
Saint James	Trinidad and Tobago
Jameseyyed	Afghanistan

JAMES SWIMMING WITH THE FISHES

James 'Whitey' Bulger is wanted by the Massachusetts State Police for Violent Fugitive Apprehension Section. Born September 3rd 1929 he is rated as a "gangster" who was once a major figure in the Boston organised crime fraternity. He is wanted after being connected with 19 murders in the Boston area during the 1970s and 1980s. There is a $2,000,000 reward for people who can supply information on this violent criminal that leads to his arrest. He features in their Top Ten Most Wanted Fugitive list.

Gangster hit man turned informant, **Aladena 'Jimmy' Fratianno** (1913-1993), started his life of crime by stealing from local markets earning him the nickname of "The Weasel". He would soon go big time and was labelled for eleven murders. He only became a grass when he learned that a rival family had put out a contract on his life.

Violent gangster **Jimmy Burke** (1931-1996) was born James Conway, and became known as 'Jimmy the Gent'. From an early age he spent much of his time in and out of jail after committing many murders, including Mafiosi killings. Robert De Niro's character James Conway in the Martin Scorsese movie *Goodfellas* (1990) is based on him.

James Cagney starred in the movie *Jimmy the Gent* in 1934 but this character was not based on Burke.

Another notable gangster was **James 'Big Jim' Colosimo** (1878-1920) who started off small time and then entered into the profitable worlds of extortion and pimping. It is estimated that along with his wife Victoria Moresco he ran over 200 brothels.

Jimmy Coonan, also known as 'Jimmy C' or 'The Big Man', was raised in the notorious Hell's Kitchen area on Manhattan's west side. He had a grudge against crime lord Mickey Spillane who had kidnapped and tortured his father when he was a youngster. Responsible for countless murders in the area he was later locked away when his one time associate Mickey Featherstone became a supergrass. He is due to be released on November 6th, 2036.

PAINTING JAMES

Irish-born painter **James Coonan** is a self-taught artist
who specialises in still life compositions. He began his
working career as an engineer but has since been able to
work on his dream job, creating paintings designed to reflect
those of the old masters.

James M. Sulkowski is a painter and sculptor who –
along with his twin brother Joseph – was commissioned in
1979 to paint murals for the Saudi Government.

At The Piano was the first major work of **James Abbott
McNeill Whistler** (1834-1903) but his most famous piece
is officially known as *The Artist's Mother* or *Arrangement in
Black and White*. We all know it as *Whistler's Mother,* which he
completed in 1871.

Though he was known more for his writing, artist **James
Ballantine** (1808-1877) actually helped to revive the art
of glass painting and was responsible for the stained glass
windows in the House of Lords.

Preferring to work with acrylic on canvas, Ghana's **James
Cudjoe**'s artwork has earned him recognition the world
over. His bold pictures contain assured strokes and dynamic
themes which have made him a favourite with collectors.

French-born artist **Jacques-Joseph Tissot** (1836-1902) is best known for his stunning paintings of English women, so much so that when he came to live in England he changed his name to James. He moved on to Biblical themes, composing over 700 paintings of Christ and scenarios from the Old Testament.

⟹⬥⬤⟸

AMERICAN PRESIDENTS NAMED JAMES

James Madison: 1809-1817
James Munroe: 1817-1825
James Knox Polk: 1845-1849
James Buchanan: 1857-1861
James Abram Garfield: 1881
Jimmy Carter (James Earl Carter): 1977-1981
As a side note, 26th President Theodore Roosevelt had an uncle called **James Alfred Roosevelt** (1825-1898) who established the Roosevelt & Son Banking House.

There have been two Vice Presidents too:

James Schoolcraft Sherman: 1909-1912
James Danforth Quayle: 1989-1993

SCARY JAMES

Writer, producer, editor and director **James Wan** gave the world one of the most successful horror franchises of all time, the stomach-churning *Saw* series. The movie actually started out as a nine-minute short but became the forefather of the horror genre known as 'torture-porn'.

Actor turned writer/director **James Gunn** has a bizarre body of work. One of his first writing credits was for *Tromeo and Juliet* (1996) he went on to appear in Troma's *Tales from the Crapper* (2004). In 2000 his novel *The Toy Collector* gained universal praise but it was his on-screen work that grabbed everyone's attention. He went on to write the scripts for blockbusters *Scooby Doo* in 2002 and its follow up *Scooby Doo 2: Monsters Unleashed* in 2004.

His re-imagining of George A Romero's *Dawn of the Dead* earned universal praise in 2004, as did his directorial effort, *Slither* in 2006.

Heroes star **James Kyson Lee** has ventured into cinema acting, predominantly in the horror genre. These include *Shutter* (2008), *Necrosis* (2008) and *The Rapture* (2009).

Another James making waves in the horror industry is Jesse James, who has appeared in the movies *Fear of the Dark* (2002), *The Butterfly Effect* (2004) and *The Amityville Horror* (2005).

One of the most controversial members of The British Board of Film Classification was **James Ferman** (1930-2002). His time as director of the BBFC ran from 1975 to 1999 and helped keep some of the most controversial films made away from British audiences. Not until he left the post were restrictions softened and Brits could enjoy uncut editions of *Evil Dead-The Ultimate Experience in Gruelling Horror* (1983), *Last House on the Left* (1972) and *The Exorcist* (1973).

Talking of exorcists, Reverend **James J. LeBar** (1936-2008) was the Chief Exorcist of the Archdiocese of New York. During his time he performed more than forty exorcisms, his most famous being a televised event held at Palm Beach, Florida. An expert on all things occult, he co-authored the best selling book *Cults, Sects and the New Age* (1989) with Father James McGuire and William Kent Burtner. LeBar was also called upon by Hollywood as a consultant on movies with exorcism content such as the Winona Ryder movie *Lost Souls* (2000).

The Disney/Pixar movie *Monsters, Inc.* (2001) had a blue furry creature named **James P. Sullivan**, who was voiced by John Goodman. Often referred to as Sulley by his colleague Mike Wazowski (Billy Crystal), he helped save a place called Monstropolis. Goodman likes to stretch his vocal chords and in the David Byrne musical *True Stories* (1986) he performs the song People Like Us. It was released as a B-Side to the Talking Heads single Wild Wild Life and earned Goodman a gold disc.

JAMES AND THE GREEN BAIZE

With nicknames such as 'Thai-Phoon' and 'The Thai Tornado', Thailand's **James Wattana** turned professional in 1989 and has won three ranking titles: 1993 Strachan Professional and the Thailand Open in 1994 and 1995. Wattana used to play standing on a crate when he was nine and seeing as though his family ran snooker clubs he had plenty of tables to practice on.

Scotsman **Jamie Burnett** is the only person to make a 148 break whilst in competition. This happened against Leo Fernandez in the qualifying rounds of the 2004 UK Travis Perkins Championship. Burnett was given a free ball and potted the brown instead of a red; he followed this with the brown again and then potted the rest of the colours in sequence but didn't manage to get 15 blacks; he had to make do with a blue and two pinks.

Another Jamie to make his name in snooker is **Jamie Jones** from Wales. He made the record books at the tender age of 14 when he became the youngest person to score 147 in a professional competition.

Jimmy 'Whirlwind' White is often referred to as 'The People's Champion'. A natural player from the age of 11, he became the youngest winner of the World Amateur Snooker Championship seven years later. He was asked by HP Sauce to change his name to James Brown in 1995 when they were sponsoring the brown coloured ball at the Masters Snooker Tournament. Jimmy has the same birthday as snooker player **Steve James** – May 2nd.

"The Welsh Potting Machine" or "The Sprog" is known on his birth certificate as **Mark James Williams**, who is not to be confused with another snooker player of the same name – Mark Williams. This one has won sixteen titles and began his sporting career wanting to be a boxer! His potting ability has made him a master of the game and earned him an MBE in 2004.

<hr/>

HO HO HO JAMES

Raymond Briggs's classic storybook *The Snowman* (published in 1978) was brought to life by TVC in 1982, with the backing of Channel 4. The story of one boy and his snowman captured the nation's hearts and has been repeated on the station every Christmas since. The famous song from the piece is Walking in the Air, which was recorded for the film by Peter Auty but it was Aled Jones who had the hit single in 1985 when it reached number five after it was recorded for a TV advert for Toys R Us. The boy in the film version was given the name **James** because animator Joanna Harrison was, at the time, dating a man called James. He later became her husband.

One Horse Open Sleigh was written by **James Lord Pierpont** (1822-1893) in 1857. He reissued it two years later under its more familiar name, Jingle Bells.

Perennial favourite Away in a Manger was first published in 1885 but has two tunes written for it. In 1887 **James Ramsey Murray** (1845-1905) composed a piece of music to accompany the lyrics whilst in 1895 a cradle-song version from William James Patrick (1838-1921) was created.

Though made famous on these shores by the Beverley Sisters in 1953, the song I Saw Mommy Kissing Santa Claus was written by Tommie Connor and originally recorded by **Jimmy Boyd** – who was just 13 at the time – in 1952. It was deemed slightly risqué as the lyrics implied that a mother was having an affair. This didn't stop it from selling millions of copies worldwide.

Tommie Connor teamed up with **Jimmy Leach** and Michael Carr in 1957 to co-write the seasonal tear-jerker The Little Boy That Santa Claus Forgot, which was made famous by Nat King Cole.

JAMES AT THE OCHE

- James 'The Machine' Wade
- James 'Lightning' Marcroft
- James 'Odd Job' Barton
- Jamie 'Bravedart' Harvey
- Jamie 'Jabba' Caven

JAMES THE GEEK

Many PCs couldn't run without the software programming language JAVA and thanks to **James Gosling** many websites are all the better for its invention. For his contribution to computer sciences he was awarded the Order of Canada in 2007.

James Gray is credited for aiding the creation of modern databases and was awarded the Turing Award for his work on transaction process technologies in 1998. He was tragically lost at sea in 2007. Another Turing Award winner was **James Hardy Wilkinson** (1915-1986) for his work on numerical analysis in 1970.

Object Modelling Techniques (OMT) and Unified Modelling Language (UML) were all created by **Dr James Rumbaugh**.

CREEPY CRAWLY JAMES

The study of insects is conducted by entomologists and there have been a number of James's in this rather specialised field.

First published in 1864, *The Entomologist's Monthly Magazine* was edited for a time by **James John Walker** (1851-1939).

James Francis Stephens (1792-1852) was an entomologist and coleopterist – people who study beetles – who helped to form The Royal Entomological Society of London in 1833.

Though he mainly studied Hemiptera and Neuroptera, Irish-born **James Nathaniel Halbert** (1871-1948) also wrote many books on the subject, the most famous of which – alongside William Frederick Johnson – was about Irish beetles.

JAMES AT THE CREASE

South African **Jacques Henry Kallis** is one of the game's finest all-rounders. In 2004 he joined Sir Donald Bradman as being the only other player to score 100 runs in five consecutive games. His first international appearance didn't indicate his batting ability. During a match against England in 1995 he was dismissed after scoring only one run.

The man regarded as the first captain of the England cricket squad was **James Lillywhite** (1842-1929). He took his team to Australia for the winter 1876-1877 tour and they drew 1-1. Lillywhite would prove to be a survivor as he outlived all the rest of his team, dying seven years after all the others had passed on. Another James, **James Southerton** (1827- 1880), played on this tour at the ripe old age of 49 and still holds the record for oldest player to debut in a Test Match.

Though Sussex player **James Langridge** (1906-1966) had a Test Match career that would span an impressive thirteen years, he only actually played eight games for England during that time. His brother John Langridge (1910-1999) also played for Sussex.

Legendary cricketer **James Charles Laker** (1922-1986) was so good that a match was actually named after him. The 'Laker' Test Match took place against Australia at Old

Trafford in 1956 where Laker captured 19 wickets, nine in the first innings and 10 in the second.

James Graham Binks was a skilled wicketkeeper but had a short international career playing just two Test Matches during the 1963-1964 English tour of India. He only missed one game out of 492 matches during his fourteen year county career for Yorkshire.

RECORD-BREAKING JAMESES

The youngest ever person to complete the Three Peaks JoGLE is **James Ellen**, 18, who finished the walk in 2008. The name derives from what the task involves, walking from **J**ohn **o'G**roats to **L**and's **E**nd whilst taking in Ben Nevis, Snowdon and Scafell Pike.

Test Match player **Jim Parks, Sr.** (1903-1980) holds the record for scoring an unbeatable 3,003 runs and capturing 101 wickets in 1937. According to *Wisden*, this will remain unless county cricket is radically changed. Jim's son, **James Park, Jr.**, also played Test cricket between 1954 and 1968.

James Milner Phillips (1905- 1974) formed part of the team that built Donald Campbell's Bluebird Proteus CN7. Phillips overlooked the construction of the car, which on July 17th 1964 reached a speed of 403.10 mph at Lake Eyre, Australia, a new land speed record at the time.

GET ALGY AND GINGER!

What-ho! Boy's own hero **James "Biggles" Bigglesworth** was created by Captain William Earl Johns (1893-1968) and had an older brother named Charles. He first appeared in a story compendium called *The Camels Are Coming* in 1932. Biggles's opening story ran fourteen pages and was entitled *The White Fokker*.

In total there were 98 Biggles books with such titles as *Biggles Follows On* (1952), *Biggles Cuts It Fine* (1954), *No Rest for Biggles* (1956), *Biggles and the Poor Rich Boy* (1961), *Biggles Sorts it Out* (1967) and *Biggles Does Some Homework* (1997).

Nobody expected it but the *Monty Python's Flying Circus* sketch the Spanish Inquisition (series two, episode two, originally broadcast in 1970) became one of their most enduring routines. Starring Michael Palin as Cardinal Ximénez, Terry Gilliam as Cardinal Fang and Terry Jones as Cardinal Biggles (complete with flying helmet) it was a send up of the real thing, just not as effective.

Biggles hit the big screen in the science fiction inspired mess that was *Biggles: Adventures in Time* (1986). Directed by John Hough and starring Neil Dickson in the title role, it bombed at the box office and any thoughts of a film franchise taking off were grounded. Sadly, it was the last film that legendary horror actor Peter Cushing (1913-1994) would appear in.

RADIO JAMES

Before The Krankies there was The Clitheroe Kid! **James Robertson Clitheroe** (1921-1973) starred in the programme about a naughty schoolboy, which ran for seventeen series from 1958 to 1972, producing 290 episodes in total.

At its peak nearly 10 million people tuned into the show. The series boasted a guest list that included Bob Monkhouse, Brian Trueman and Judith Chalmers! James himself stood at only 4ft 3ins but was actually from Clitheroe.

Another short James, **Little Jimmy Dickens** (real name James Cecil Dickens) was just 4ft 11ins and sang at the Grand Ole Opry for nearly 60 years. Though his repertoire was mainly constructed of comedy and novelty songs he gained respect from more serious singers. His famous hit was May The Bird Of Paradise Fly Up Your Nose from the album I'm Little, But I'm Loud. It never charted in the UK.

Outspoken and controversial radio presenter **James Whale** (b. 1951) – real first name Michael – has had a colourful career. He created the first ever in-store radio station in 1970, Topshop Radio, but is best known as a radio phone-in host. He began at Metro Radio in 1974, hosting the famous *Nightowls* show and in the early 1990s combined the radio and TV mediums by hosting the late night series *The James Whale Radio Show* on ITV. Most recently he was fired from Talksport for hinting to listeners to vote for Boris Johnson during London's Mayoral Elections.

Count Jim Moriarty was one of Spike Milligan's creations for the radio series *The Goons* (1951-1960). Spike, real name Terrence Milligan (1918-2002) also played the characters **Jim Spriggs** – who called everyone "Jim" – and **Little Jim** who only ever said; "He's fallen in the water".

⋙◈⋘

JAMES IN BUSINESS

One of the most aptly named Jameses is **James Cash Penney** (1875-1971) who was born in Caldwell County, Missouri. A born entrepreneur, he raised his own livestock to pay for his clothing as his father encouraged him (and his other eleven siblings) to know exactly the value of money. James would go on to open his own store under the name J.C. Penney on April 14th, 1902. It would take only a year for him to open another two. At the moment there are 1,067 J.C. Penney stores in the US.

James Wolfensohn (born 1933) became the ninth president of the World Bank Group in 1995 and held the position for ten years. During his tenure he strove for reform and helped highlight the plight of the poor around the world.

Formed by William Procter and **James Norris Gamble** (1803-1891) in 1837, Procter and Gamble is one of the world's biggest companies. Born in Enniskillen, Ireland, Gamble earned his money by making soap and his son, also called James (1836-1932), helped develop their most famous product, Ivory Soap. The product became famous because it floated on water – an apparent error during production meant that a batch of the soap was whipped for a longer period than normal! True or not, the first advertising campaign in 1891 bore the legend 'It floats' which helped it sell by the case load.

Mystery still surrounds the whereabouts of **Jimmy Hoffa**, a union leader who disappeared on July 30th, 1975. He was leader of The International Brotherhood of Teamsters who represented fire fighters and truck drivers. He had connections with the Mafia but rumour has it he fell out with the organised crime syndicate and Hoffa went to prison in 1967 for fraud. He served just over four years and was released on the understanding that he had to stay away from union matters until 1980. Danny DeVito directed a movie about his life in 1992. Simply called *Hoffa*, Jack Nicholson played the lead role and was nominated for two Oscars. Ironically, Jimmy's middle name was Riddle.

TRAGIC JAMES

The adopted son of James Cagney, **James Cagney Jr.**, sadly died, aged only 44, from a heart attack.

Respected actor **James Hazeldine** had carved himself a notable career as a serious actor appearing in such TV shows as *The Omega Factor* (1979), *Chocky* (1984) and *Shipman* (2002). His stint on ITV drama series *London's Burning* (1988-96) as Mike Wilson gained him a legion of female fans. He died aged only 55 after contracting septicaemia after heart surgery.

James Dandu Maligisa, or **James Maligisa Dandu** to some, was born in 1970 and released his first album in 1992. Also known as Cool James, CJ Massive and Mtoto wa Dandu he was a Tanzanian who excelled in producing dance music. He was killed in a car accident in Dar es Salaam in 2002.

Jim Fixx (1932-1984) wrote the bestseller, *The Complete Book of Running* which was published in 1977. In the book, Jim informs the reader how running helps to lead a healthy life. Unfortunately, Jim died of a heart attack while out jogging; he was only 52.

There is an urban legend called 'The Steam Tunnel Incident'. It concerns players who die playing live versions of the fantasy game *Dungeons & Dragons*. Actually, all are based on one tragic event. In 1979 **James Dallas Egbert III** was pressured by his parents to achieve and became addicted to drugs.

Egbert rarely played D & D and whilst attending Michigan State University decided to end it all. He entered the steam tunnels with suicide on his mind, leaving a map behind to show his location. The suicide attempt failed and he left the tunnels and ran away leaving all his belongings. The next morning his stuff was found but James had disappeared. Rumours grew that the game was to blame and he had disappeared playing some live version of it. It gets cloudy here as various reports cropped up and theories started to emerge: some libellous, others just bizarre.

Private Investigator William Dear followed the case and found Egbert. By the time the PI had caught up with James, he had once again attempted suicide. Dear agreed not to tell anyone the true facts and James became the custody of his uncle, Dr Marvin Goss. Sadly on August 16th, 1980 James died from a self-inflicted gunshot wound. In 1984 William Dear released a book about the case, *The Dungeon Master*.

Baby Huey, aka **James Ramsey**, had a poor start to life. He was born with a glandular problem that caused him to be seriously overweight from a young age. This didn't stop his musical ambitions and in 1963 he formed Baby Huey and the Babysitters. Ramsey signed his first major deal in 1969, without the band. He then became addicted to heroin and his ever-escalating weight caused him to die of a heart attack in 1970, at the age of just 26. His first album, The Baby Huey Story: The Living Legend was released posthumously in 1971.

ONE CLUB JAMES

There have been a number of footballers who have spent their entire professional career at one club:

Name	Club	Date	Pos.	Apps (Gls)
Jim Barrett Sr.	West Ham United	1924-1939	Centre Half	467 (53)
Jimmy Dickinson	Portsmouth	1946-1965	Left Half	764 (9)
Jim Hammond	Fulham	1928-1939	Forward	342 (150)
Glyn James	Blackpool	1960-1975	Defender	399 (22)

⬤◆⬤

ENGLAND ONE-CAP WONDERS:

Name	Date	Opposition
James Prinsep	1879	Scotland
James Ward	1885	Wales
James Conlin	1906	Scotland
Jim Barrett	1928	N. Ireland
Jimmy Hagan	1948	Denmark
Jimmy Meadows	1955	Scotland

JAMES IN SPRINGFIELD

The Simpsons is one of the most successful TV shows ever and after 20 seasons and a hit movie there is no sign of it stopping – just yet.

Here's a selection of Springfield Jameses.

Jimbo Jones:
School bully, voiced mainly by Pamela Hayden, who wears a woollen hat and skull T-shirt. His first name is Corky.
Jacques:
Bowling instructor voiced by Albert Brooks.
Cooter:
Voiced by **Jim Varney**, he was a Carnival man who duped Homer.
Jim Hope:
Toy Executive voiced by Tim Robbins.
Lucky Jim:
Bail bondsman voiced by Robert Foster.

In the first *Tree House of Horror* episode, **James Earl Jones** played Narrator, Mover and Serak and in *Tree House of Horror V*, Maggie Simpson. He popped up again in the episode *Das Bus*.

James Woods, **James Caan** and **James L. Brooks**, **James Patterson** and **Jim Jarmusch** have all played themselves.

Comic book James

Hairy, metal skeleton mutant **James Howlett** is better known as his alter ego Wolverine, a member of the *X-Men* which is published by Marvel Comics. He first full appearance was in issue 181 of *The Incredible Hulk* – although he did pop up in one frame of issue 180 – and was created by Len Wein and John Romita, Sr. He's probably one of the shortest superheroes ever measuring at only 5ft 3ins. Another Marvel wolf hero is **John Jameson**, a former astronaut who now has the tag Man-Wolf.

James Proudstar (also known as Thunderbird) holds a grudge against X-Men leader Professor Xavier as his brother, the original Thunderbird (John Proudstar), died on a mission.

Engineer **Dr James MacDonald Hudson** now goes by the slightly pompous name of The Guardian.

Superman's ginger haired, freckle-faced, photographer side-kick **Jimmy Olsen** got his own spin-off comic in 1954. Simply entitled *Superman's Pal Jimmy Olsen* it ran for 163 issues. In 1993, the Spin Doctors reached number 40 in the British charts with the single Jimmy Olsen's Blues.

It's a family affair for Kid Quantum in the DC comic universe. When **James Cullen** joined The Legion of Superheroes and became Kid Quantum he battled an alien named Tangleweb and bit the dust. His sister Jazmin stepped into his lycra pants and became Kid Quantum II.

JAMES IN THE SCRUM

James Peters (1879-1954) was the first black rugby union player to play for the English side. Born in Salford to West Indian parents, Peters proved himself to be an able athlete whilst at school and went on to play for Knowle Rugby Club and Devon Rugby Club, which led to his England selection in 1906. Bigots and racists dogged his career but he proved himself a strong member of the international set-up. His career came to a halt in 1910 when he was involved in an accident in a dockyard where three fingers were severed from one of his hands. Two years later he played rugby league for Barrow, and then St Helens.

Gloucester wing and centre **James Simpson-Daniel** was named Guinness Premiership Player of the Year for the 2007/08 season. He earned 10 England caps in six years but has been beset with a spate of unfortunate injuries, including back, shoulder and thigh problems, as well as glandular fever and viral infections.

Welsh rugby star **Carwyn James** (1929-1983) once said; "Get your retaliation in first". Very wise words when playing the sport! A sports building at the University of Wales is named in his honour.

Another Welsh rugby star is **John James Williams,** who earned thirty caps. After his rugby career ended he moved into business creating JJ Williams Painting Services and formed part of the consortium that put in a bid to construct the Millennium Stadium. James is still associated with sport; his three children have also represented Wales in track and field events.

JAMES THE BRAVE

The Victoria Cross is awarded to those who show immense courage in the face of adversity and can be awarded posthumously. The bearer may use the initial VC after their name.

The cross has been awarded to many brave Jameses, here are just a few:

James Power Carne – Gloucestershire Regiment
James Collis – Royal Horse Artillery
James Craig – Scots Fusilier Guards
James Langly Dalton – Commissariat and Transport Department
Robert James Thomas Digby-Jones – Royal Engineers
James Dundas – Bengal Engineers
James Firth – The Duke of Wellington's Regiment
James Gorman – Royal Navy
James Hills – Bengal Horse Artillery
James John McLeod Innes – Bengal Engineers
James McKechnie – Scots Fusilier Guards
Thomas James Young – Royal Navy

There is every chance we have missed a James, or two.

Let us know at **www.stripepublishing.co.uk**

ACKNOWLEDGMENTS

First of all huge thanks must go to Dan Tester and his team for giving me the chance to prove myself and for allowing a rookie to join in the fun.

To my family and friends, cheers for putting up with my absence at gatherings and functions, now you know what I've been up to over the last six months!

But biggest thanks goes to my wife Clare for listening to me talk constantly about the project and writing long into the night.

And to those Jameses mentioned in this book, thanks to you all.

BIBLIOGRAPHY

Books

Halliwell's Film Guide – Harper Collins 23rd Revised Edition 2007

Halliwell's Who's Who in the Movies – John Walker - Harper Collins 2006

British Hit Singles and Albums (Guinness 20th Revised Edition) 2007

The Concise Oxford English Dictionary – OUP Oxford 11th Revised Edition 2008

Doctor Who: The Television Companion – David J. Howe and Stephen James Walker – BBC Books 1998

Doctor Who: Encyclopaedia – Gary Russell BBC Books 2007

Recommended websites

www.imdb.com
www.bbc.co.uk
www.royal.gov.uk
www.nasa.gov
www.catholic.org
www.number10.gov.uk
www.sitcom.co.uk
www.thebiographychannel.co.uk
www.lordmayorsshow.org
www.fbi.gov
www.whitehouse.gov
www.nba.com
www.britishcomedy.org.uk
www.cricinfo.com
www.wikipedia.org